The Transforming Vision
Shaping a Christian World View

Brian J. Walsh

J. Richard Middleton

Foreword by Nicholas Wolterstorff

InterVarsity Press
Downers Grove
Illinois 60515

InterVarsity Press is the book-publishing division of Inter-Varsity Christian Fellowship, a student movement active on campus at hundreds of universities, colleges and schools of nursing. For information about local and regional activities, write IVCF, 233 Langdon St., Madison, WI 53703.

Distributed in Canada through InterVarsity Press, 860 Denison St., Unit 3, Markham, Ontario L3R 4H1, Canada.

Scripture quotations, unless otherwise noted, are taken from the Holy Bible: New International Version. Copyright © 1978 by the New York International Bible Society. Used by permission of Zondervan Bible Publishers.

Scripture quotations marked KJV are from the King James Version of the Bible. Those marked NASB are from the New American Standard Bible, © The Lockman Foundation 1960, 1962, 1963, 1968, 1971, 1972, 1973, 1975, 1977. Used by permission.

The lyrics on page 140 are taken from "The Candy Man's Gone" written by Bruce Cockburn, © 1982 Golden Mountain Music Corp. (taken from the True North album "The Trouble with Normal"). Used by permission.

Cover illustration: John Walker

ISBN 0-87784-973-0

Printed in the United States of America

Library of Congress Cataloging in Publication Data

Walsh, Brian J., 1953-
    The transforming vision.

    Bibliography: p.
    1. Christianity—Philosophy.   2. Christianity and culture.   3. Identification (Religion)   4. Civilization, Modern—20th century.   I. Middleton, J. Richard.
    II. Title.
    BR100.W35   1984   201   84-15646
    ISBN 0-87784-973-0 (pbk.)

19   18   17   16   15   14   13   12   11   10   9   8   7   6   5   4   3   2
99   98   97   96   95   94   93   92   91   90   89   88   87   86   85

*To our students and
the Institute for Christian Studies*

Foreword

A deep disappointment and a profound longing motivate this book. The authors, themselves Christians, observe that vast numbers of their fellow North Americans count themselves as Christians. Yet Christianity is ineffective in shaping our public life. What effectively shapes our public life and our society generally is our adulation of science and technology and economic growth. Christianity for the most part stands in the wings and watches. That is their disappointment. Their longing is that things may be changed—that Christianity may receive social and cultural embodiment. For in this they see the life and guidance and hope that our society so badly needs.

Walsh and Middleton ask why the Christianity of North Americans remains so disembodied. Their answer goes something like this: If we probe any society for what it is that primarily forms that society, we discover it is the *world view* of those who compose that society. This shapes their existence. A people's world view is their way of thinking about life and the world, coupled with the values they set for themselves in the context of that way of thinking. The Japanese have a world view which shapes their lives together, the Canadian Dene Indians have one, the majority culture in North America has one, and so forth.

There is also a Christian world view, not indeed embodied clearly in any extant society but expressed in the Scriptures. To adopt Christianity with authenticity is to be a person of faith who embraces that biblical world view. Walsh and Middleton give a fresh statement of what that biblical world view is. They wish especially to emphasize that an accurate scrutiny of this world view makes clear its comprehensiveness. This is a world view for shaping all of life and not just for shaping some "religious" or "spiritual" or "sacred" corner of life.

So why doesn't it actually work this way? Why does the Christian world view remain so disembodied in spite of the fact that so many in our society count themselves as Christians? The answer that Walsh and Middleton develop is that Christians in general fail to perceive the radical comprehensiveness of the biblical world view. They assume that its formative impact does not reach beyond some "religious" corner of life. "Lo, here but not there" is how they think. They fail to perceive the longing of God for the expression of faith in the *polis*. Accordingly some other, competing, world view and some other, competing, faith shape their public lives. Christians, in short, are dualists.

This book, then, is a passionate call to Christians to be of one heart and mind and to acknowledge that Jesus Christ is Lord in all of life. Read it as a provocative analysis of what hinders such singleness of heart and mind. Read it also as a provocative prescription for overcoming the hindrance and recovering the service of just one Master.

Nicholas Wolterstorff
Calvin College

Preface

This book originated in some twenty courses on the Christian world
view which the two of us taught on assorted university campuses in
Southern Ontario between 1977 and 1983. Our aim was to help students
develop an integrated Christian world view, a world view both faithful
to the Scriptures and motivating for Christian obedience in a secular
age. This book has the same goal.

Part 1 will introduce world views. Chapter one discusses what they
are and how they affect us. In chapter two we look at ways of evaluating
them: What makes a particular world view good? From this overview
we move in Part 2 to an explanation of the biblical world view. Each of
the three chapters here develops a crucial element of the Christian perspective. Part 3, "The Modern World View," lays out the vision that
now guides Western society. Chapter six notes its dualistic base, and
chapter seven explains where it came from. Chapters eight and nine
analyze the idolatry and predicament of our present age.

Parts 1 to 3 prepare us for the Christian response of Part 4. In these last chapters we emphasize the communal nature of our cultural response. The conclusions reached here bear particularly on Christians in scholarship, and thus the bibliography with which we close is much more than an add-on. It is indeed a bibliography we can't live without.

Our belief that world views are communal is indicated by the fact that this book is coauthored. But the communal nature of this book is also evidenced by the many others who contributed to the project. Unfortunately we can thank only a few in this space.

Hendrik Hart, James Olthuis and Al Wolters, professors at the Institute for Christian Studies, Toronto, have had a profound influence on our thinking. Robert Vandervennen, director of educational services at the Institute for Christian Studies, has supported and encouraged the project from the beginning.

Don Sedgwick's editorial assistance on the initial draft of the manuscript was invaluable. Susan Bower, Jack Kuhatschek, Jane Wells and Jim Sire read the whole manuscript and offered helpful comments. The manuscript was typed by Don Knudsen and Kathy Vanderkloet. Gord Carkner and Ruth Irwin assisted in compiling the bibliography. And the Institute for Christian Studies generously provided needed financial assistance. We are deeply indebted to all of these for participating in this communal project.

But there is a special kind of communal participation that we want to note. Wendy Bartley and Marcia Middleton did not type the manuscript or offer editorial advice. They simply loved us. We thank Yahweh, our Lord, for that love and for his constant, covenantal faithfulness to us.

Finally, this book would never have been written without our students. Their questions, insights and enthusiastic responses to the Christian world view and its life-transforming implications constituted a major impetus in our writing.

Brian Walsh
Richard Middleton
Montreal, Christmas 1983.

PART 1

What Are World Views?

CHAPTER 1

World View
and Culture

Anthony sat and talked to us in the brightly lit coffee shop for a long time. Although we could understand his problem, it seemed impossible for us to touch it. We could not bridge the perceptual gulf between us. It was the kind of gulf that separates two ways of life, two world views.

Anthony had come to Canada to study commerce, intending to return home to Singapore and go into business. On his return he was to marry a girl he had had a relationship with for some years. Although they were not officially engaged, it was assumed within their cultural setting that they would marry.

But something happened. In his second year in Canada Anthony became a Christian through the Inter-Varsity Christian Fellowship group on his campus. He began to grow as a person in ways he had never anticipated. As often happens during such periods of growth, old plans began to change. Anthony concluded that he was not in love with his friend back home, and he began to cool the relationship in his letters. Finally it became necessary to go home and make a clean break.

As Anthony told his story, we were impressed with the moral integrity of both what he had done and how he had done it. Now that he had returned, however, Anthony was a broken and depressed young man. Because he had ended this relationship, his family had rejected him. "You are worse than an animal," his father had said. "Even animals show gratitude."

In his parents' eyes and in the eyes of his former girlfriend's parents, Anthony had committed an unpardonable sin. He had dashed the hopes and expectations of his family by being disloyal to a woman to whom he had been betrothed. In Anthony's home culture, loyalty is one of the highest of all moral duties.

This story illustrates in a painful way the pervasive character of world views. Anthony's family "saw" what he had done completely differently from how we "saw" it. What stood out for us was Anthony's integrity of character. We saw a young man who refused to hide behind the thousands of miles which separated him from an unpleasant situation. We saw a young man both open and sensitive in the way he related to his former girlfriend. If his parents had noticed these admirable characteristics in Anthony, they certainly did not see their importance. They saw primarily a lack of loyalty and gratitude.

We have here two different ways of seeing—indeed, two world views. What made the situation even more painful, however, was that the two world views were at war within Anthony himself. Although some people might claim otherwise, conversion to Jesus Christ does not immediately wipe out years of being raised according to another religious vision. Anthony knew that as a Christian his actions were loving and honest, but in his Eastern heart the accusations of his parents still struck home. Perhaps he really was the scoundrel that his father said he was!

This world view battle, this fundamentally spiritual tension, plagued and depressed Anthony for months. The best we could do as Christian friends was to affirm the Christian side of that battle. We tried to raise his self-esteem by assuring him of his worth in the eyes of his Lord and of his Christian sisters and brothers.

This book is about world views. World views are best understood as we see them incarnated, fleshed out in actual ways of life. They are not systems of thought, like theologies or philosophies. Rather, world views are perceptual frameworks. They are ways of seeing. If we want to understand what people see, or how well people see, we need to watch how they walk. If they bump into certain objects or stumble over them, then we can assume that they are blind to them. Conversely, their eyes may not only see but dwell on certain other objects.

Two examples will illustrate the point. First we will look at how child-rearing practices in Japan differ from those in Canada and then we will contrast the views of land held by North America's dominant culture and by its native Indian culture.

On Bathing Babies

In 1959 anthropologist Margaret Mead helped produce a film entitled *The Four Families*.[1] The film portrays a day in the life of four families from four different cultures: India, France, Japan and Canada. The families are farming families of roughly equivalent social and class status. The contrast between the Japanese and the Canadian families is especially intriguing.

The Japanese family is extended; the paternal grandparents live with the family of the oldest son. The baby spends most of her time on the grandmother's back—a sight still common in the oriental communities of large North American cities. In the film the advice of the grandparents holds authority. The grandma's wisdom is especially important in child-rearing. Indeed, Mead notes that the mother is dominated by her mother-in-law. When it comes time for the baby's bath, the mother hands the baby to the grandmother in the huge tub; grandmother holds the baby close to her body and washes it. Lemons float in the water to protect them from evil.

In the home are both Shinto and Buddhist shrines, before which the adults perform short religious ceremonies, worshiping the gods and ancestors. The children share delicate, carefully manufactured toys. Neither the brother nor the sister can claim to own any toys individually.

At the end of the film a Japanese resource person was asked what characteristics were socialized into Japanese children. She answered that they should become docile, gentle, obedient, submissive and dependent. Now look at the Canadian family. What immediately strikes us is that the children in this nuclear family are encouraged to develop self-sufficiency, self-reliance and independence. Each child has his or her toys and is taught to respect the other's property rights. When one child (a boy) bites his tongue at supper, he is admonished not to be a crybaby. In addition, the religious ceremony of saying grace before the meal is performed not by a parent but by one of the children.

Most interesting is the baby's bath. The ritual is performed with great efficiency. It seems almost a medical event as the baby's nose and ears are painfully probed with cotton swabs. Rather than being in the tub experiencing the closeness of a parent, the baby is on her own. Noting that the mother struggles with the baby for the washcloth, Mead comments, "Again, the emphasis on independence, assertiveness and the development of will power." While the Japanese baby (like French and Indian children) is breast-fed and put to sleep with a lullaby, the Canadian baby has been weaned early. At bedtime she is given her bottle and placed in the crib. The light is turned off and the door shut. No lullaby.

Of course, not every Japanese and Canadian family lives exactly as the ones in this film. Too, the film dates back to a time when family roles in Japan were more traditional and when Benjamin Spock's *Baby and Child Care* was the bible for many young baby-boom families in North America. Yet these two families' living patterns do shed light on the nature of the world view differences between the two cultures.

When we look at a culture, we are looking at the pieces of a puzzle. We can see the functioning of assorted institutions, like the family, government, schools, cultic institutions (churches, temples, synagogues and so on) and businesses. We can observe different modes of recreation, different sports, transportation and eating habits. Each culture develops a unique artistic and musical life. All of these cultural activities are pieces of the puzzle.

The question is, How do we put the puzzle together? How do the pieces interrelate? What is the pattern of the culture? Is there a key that unlocks the pattern? Yes. The central element which brings the pieces of the puzzle together into a coherent whole is the world view that has the leading role in the life of that culture.

So, if we are to truly understand why a Japanese family is so different from a Canadian family (or why Anthony had to suffer so much in breaking off his relationship), we need to understand the distinctive world views that are in force. Why is the grandmother so important in Japan and other Eastern cultures? Why does she have the honor of bathing the baby? Why must the children share their delicate and aesthetically rich toys? Why are children raised to be docile, gentle, submissive and dependent? Although each of these questions has many answers, we will understand the Japanese way of life better if we know more about their vision of life.

The Supreme People

The traditional Japanese world view was formed by three ancient religious traditions: Shintoism, Confucianism and Buddhism. These religions do not compete with each other in Japan. Rather they come together to form the dominant vision of life for that culture. In their curriculum book entitled *Japan: A Way of Life,* authors Arnold De-Graaff, Jean Olthuis and Anne Tuininga offer this insight:

> All three formal religions of Japan emphasize a sense of group loyalty and of obligation to superiors. To practice these as a way of life requires self-denial and self-control. The individual person tends to deny his or her personal needs and desires and to lose himself or herself in the interests of the group. He or she receives a sense of personal importance by being a loyal member of the group. Therefore no one can do without the group's support and approval.[2]

Selfishness is seen to destroy the original harmony between man and nature, man and man, and man and himself. Loyalty to the group is the only way to regain that harmony because such loyalty leaves no place for selfishness. And what is the group?

The group is, in the first place, the family. "Bringing dishonor upon the family name is the worst thing a person can do."[3] Such dishonor shows both disloyalty and ingratitude to one's superiors in the family hierarchy. Loyalty and gratitude also extend to ancestors. According to DeGraaff, Olthuis and Tuininga, the family is "formed by a line of descent unbroken through the centuries. The spirit of every ancestor lives on, and is still part of the family."[4] The worship of ancestors, or filial piety, is central to the Japanese way of life.

But the ultimate family is not just the line of descent of a particular extended family. It is the nation as a whole. The Japanese have a traditional belief that they are the direct descendants of the sun-goddess *Amaterasu-Omi-Kami*. Such descent destines them to be the supreme people of the world. Therefore, the final place of loyalty is to the nation.

All these facets are integral to the Japanese vision of life. Although far from comprehensive, they shed some light on the Japanese and oriental way of life. The place of the grandparents in the family is firmly established as long as traditional filial piety is fostered. And children will not need to protect their own toys because they will be socialized to be humble and submissive. For religious reasons they instill gentleness, obedience, docility and dependence—because selfishness is the root of all disharmony and because the national family must come to world preeminence. This can only happen if the people are loyal.

This religious sense of loyalty was at the root of the Japanese activities in World War 2. No other nation in that war could expect the kind of self-sacrificial loyalty that was common among the Japanese military forces. After the humiliating defeat in 1945, the honor of Japan became staked on Japan's eventual economic superiority over the Western world. Postwar industrialization was a religious attempt to regain national pride.

The shape that such industrialization took, however, has been different from that of Western capitalism. Because of its religious vision of life, Japan can count on a dedicated and loyal work force. The industrial enterprise is not an individualistic battle between management and labor, but a national endeavor. Workers relate to the corporation with the loyalty that characterizes all of their lives. Employment is for life, not a commodity to be sold to the highest bidder in the labor market.

This fundamental sense of loyalty and gratitude also accounts for the hurt Anthony experienced, for the world views of Japan and Singapore have similar roots. Breaking a relationship was not merely a personal matter in the relationship between a man and a woman; it had deep religious ramifications.

Since a later chapter will deal with the North American and Western world view in some detail, we can be brief in our discussion of the Canadian family here. The contrast with the Japanese family is clear. The values instilled in the Canadian children—independence, individuality and self-reliance—are almost the direct opposite of the Japanese values of dependence, loyalty and obedience. The baby is not granted the indulgence of her mother's breast or a lullaby before bed. She is on her own, holding her own bottle; she is expected to go to sleep like adults when the light is turned off. And children are given more freedom, whether in talking back or in struggling for a face cloth.

Why are Canadian children raised like this? The Judeo-Christian heritage, with its emphasis on God's concern for us as individual persons, is one of the reasons. Human beings have value and are important in the sight of God. But there are other reasons as well, for the individualism of the Western world view is contrary to the biblical notions of community, service and the body of Christ. The West emphasizes the individual because it sees persons as autonomous. The Renaissance championed the self-made man. The North American pioneer spirit champions the person who makes it on his or her own, the one who is assertive and self-reliant.

Contemporary North American life demands that people have these qualities. Business life, for example, is not a life of loyalty to a company, meant to enhance the national honor. North Americans participate in corporations with no national obligations at all—they are, in fact, multinational corporations. The purpose of work is to create economic security and material affluence primarily for individuals and nuclear families. If another corporation offers more money and better benefits, the wage earner overlooks loyalty and gratitude to accept the new job.

Such a society needs aggressive individuals, not loyal group members. Without the force of filial piety, grandparents in such an individualistic society usually live apart from their children. When they can no longer care for themselves, elderly people are "placed" in institutions to be cared for by professionals. In such a society the elderly become useless and are consequently discarded. No longer economically productive, they are, it is assumed, too old to offer meaningful advice to their children in the modern world. Little wonder that Japanese and Canadian children have such different relationships with their grandparents!

The contrast between the traditional Japanese way of life and the Canadian way of life gives evidence of two different world views. One has its roots in Buddhist, Shinto and Confucian beliefs about the group, ancestors, the sun-goddess, loyalty and gratitude, while the other has its roots in a mixture of Christian and humanist beliefs about the individual, autonomy and economic progress. These visions of life lead their respective adherents into radically different ways of life.

And these world view differences can been seen in such a mundane event as giving a baby her bath. It may strike Westerners as an odd superstition to place lemons in a tub to protect a family from evil, but we could ask whether the aura of scientific, medical hygiene that surrounds *our* bathing of babies is not just as religious, perhaps even superstitious.

A Pluralism of World Views
The Japanese and Canadian family lifestyles illustrate the world view difference between two geographically and politically distinct cultures. But not all members of either society accept the dominant world view and the common way of life of their respective cultures. Minority world views and alternative communities are always present in any society. Indeed, the early Christian church was just such an alternative community during the Roman era.

When society manifests a plurality of world views, problems arise. If no one vision is dominant, that society becomes a house divided against itself, and inevitably it will experience cultural disintegration. But when there is a majority position, when one world view dominates the others, the culture must somehow deal with the minorities. The issue is significant ethically and politically. How does the mainline society, with its allegiance to the culturally dominant vision of life, relate to the minority groups within it?

The Christians of the first century A.D. rudely discovered how the dominant culture would deal with their alternative community when Nero ordered their persecution. The fascist world view of Hitler led to the attempted elimination of the Jewish race. Examples of dominant cultures crushing their minority groups abound even today in the totalitarian regimes of the left and right.

The question of pluralism has been a central issue also for colonial nations, except that the situation is reversed. In the case of colonialism the question is not how the majority deals with a minority, but how a powerful colonial minority deals with the aboriginal majority which it has "colonialized." Colonialism creates the odd situation where the new world view of the colonial power is forced on the majority population of the colony. We see an extreme example of this in the racist apartheid policies of South Africa.

South Africa is not, however, the only country in the world that has a "native problem." So do Canada and the United States. Both of these nations are colonial in the sense that they are inhabited and ruled by people of primarily European (that is, foreign) heritage. But people were here before the Europeans arrived, and they are still here today. The native peoples of North America had a world view and a way of life before the white settlers came, and that world view contrasts with the European vision of life as strongly as does the Japanese world view. From the very beginning of the European conquest of North America there has been world view pluralism, and hence a world view problem.

How did the colonial powers attempt to deal with that pluralism? They tried to assimilate the native population into the melting pot of Western culture. If the native peoples did not want to be assimilated into white culture (and the attitudes of whites made such assimilation almost impossible), then they were given two options: either death in battle, or isolation on reservations where their way of life could not be continued. The second option amounted to cultural destruction (some would say genocide) as much as the first, but the process was slower.

Sir John A. Macdonald, Canada's first prime minister, made it clear that the dominant European culture would leave no political, cultural or

economic room for the aboriginal peoples of the continent: "The Indians and Metis [half-breeds] of the Northwest will be held down with a
firm hand till the west is over-run and controlled by white settlers."⁵
Hollywood westerns show us that American domestic policy was the
same as Canada's.

The insistence on assimilation was an outright rejection of cultural
pluralism. Thomas Berger, commissioner of a recent Canadian government inquiry into proposals to build a pipeline through the Mackenzie
Valley in Canada's Northwest Territories, made this observation: "It
was to be the white man's mission not only to tame the land and bring it
under cultivation, but also to tame the native people and bring them
within the pale of civilization."⁶ A number of assumptions are, of course,
implicit here: (1) natives are savages who need taming; (2) native culture
is not a civilization; and (3) native customs are inferior to those of the
European colonists and have to be rejected.

The supposed inferiority of the native way of life led most Christian missionaries to bring both the gospel of Jesus Christ *and* the civilization of Europe to the native peoples. In Canada, for example, the church
took control of native education. It viewed education as the most effective way to loose the Indians from their traditional lifestyle and to begin
to incorporate them into the dominant white culture. It is no wonder that so many natives today (and national peoples throughout the
world who have come into contact with Christian missionaries) simply equate Christianity with Western culture. And they categorically
reject both.

Most of the Indian children in the Northwest Territories boarded
at the schools where they were being educated. In 1893 Mr. Hayter
Reed, superintendent of Indian Affairs, made their purpose clear: "In
the boarding or industrial schools the pupils are removed for a long
time from the leadings of this uncivilized life and receive constant
care and attention."⁷ By removing the children from their parents,
dressing them in the clothes common to the southern whites and
banning the use of native languages and native religious observances,
whites hoped that these children would reject their traditional world
view and way of life and be converted to white civilization.

Although this assimilative program did manage to create children with little self-esteem (they were taught to be ashamed of their native cultural heritage), and although it did produce young people who had lost their traditional skills of hunting, fishing and trapping, it did not produce brown people integrated into white culture. Native people had lost their language, religion and way of life, but they had not been able to truly adopt the white world view.

Caught between two cultures, they became a disillusioned and broken people, not so different from young Anthony. Rootless and spiritually homeless, many came to depend on government welfare. The stereotype of the drunken, lazy Indian has its origins in this world view crisis. Ironically, the only commodity that receives government subsidy in the Canadian Northwest Territories, making its price as low as the south's, is liquor.[8] While food and clothing are expensive, alcohol is relatively cheap. The rationale of the Canadian government is hard to understand.

Looking at Land

In the last fifteen years the native peoples of North America have begun to do something about their plight. Integral to the renewal, or even the survival, of their culture is a return to their traditional world view and way of life. Native spirituality has made a marked resurgence. Indians are saying that the only way they can regain control over their lives and free themselves from dependence on both government welfare and alcohol is by returning to their traditional values.

Central to these values is the native view of the land. Their view of land, however, brings them immediately into spiritual, legal and political conflict with the dominant society of Canada. Thomas Berger pinpoints the problem. The conflict is between those who view land as a frontier (the Europeans) and those who view it as a homeland (the Dene and Inuit). Berger writes:

We look upon the North as a frontier. It is natural for us to think of developing it, of subdividing the land and extracting its resources to fuel Canada's industry and heat our homes. Our whole inclination is to think of expanding our industrial machine to the limit of our country's frontiers. . . . But the native people say the North is their homeland. They have lived there for thousands of years. They claim it is their land, and they believe they have a right to say what its future ought to be.[9]

Now our white colonial society has never allowed the native people to freely maintain their way of life. But the problem becomes acute when the Indians' way of life actually obstructs the path of *our* way of life. This occurs most noticeably when we need to use Indian land for our own industrial purposes. At issue may be a power dam, a logging project or the exploration and transportation of oil and natural gas.[10]

Although such conflict inevitably leads to debate on the legal question of native land claims, the issue is not primarily legal or political. On a most fundamental level the issue is one of contrasting world views. Economist E. F. Schumacher once said, "Study how a society uses its land, and you can come to pretty reliable conclusions as to what its future will be."[11] We could also say that a society's future is dependent on its vision, and its vision can be ascertained from observing how it uses its land.

Why do Euro-Canadians view the north as a frontier while the Dene and Inuit peoples view it as a homeland? It is not enough merely to say that it is a frontier for us because we are relatively recent arrivals in North America, while the natives see it as a homeland because they've been here longer. Undoubtedly those historical realities are relevant, but there is more.

Western culture characteristically views humanity in an "over-against" relation to nature. Schumacher says, "Modern man does not experience himself as a part of nature but as an outside force destined to dominate and conquer it."[12] Nature is a threat. It is wild and irrational. It must therefore be tamed, domesticated and subjected to rational control by humans. Moreover, "nature is the domain of man's self-realization."[13] That is to say, in our manipulation and exploitation of nature we build our society, which is our self-assertion. Key here is the notion of exploitation. Nature exists to be exploited by humans; apart from that it has little value.

A recent television commercial from Imperial Oil (Exxon) illustrates the antagonistic and exploitative character of our relation to nature. Men are working on an oil rig in the Beaufort Sea. The announcer impresses on us how unfavorable the conditions of this arctic sea are for human beings. To exploit the vast oil fields under the ocean floor is a difficult and dangerous task. Oil rigs strain visibly against the gale-force arctic winds. Supply barges, bobbing corks in a raging sea, spend tedious hours trying to dock with the chilling platform. All is encased in ice. But the technology of Imperial Oil will conquer this ocean and bring oil to southern Canada to ensure that we will not freeze in the dark this winter.

Nature here is seen as the constant adversary. We take from nature, by means of our labor and technology, the resources we consume to insulate ourselves from nature. The commercial exudes confidence that mankind can conquer and exploit nature. That an oil spill would be impossible to clean up under these conditions and would result in untold ecological damage is, of course, not mentioned.

In the Western view resources can be owned as well as exploited. Not only can they be owned, but they can also be bought and sold. Land is a market commodity just like food and clothing. That might not strike us as very odd, but it is worth noting that the idea of selling land is a relatively new idea even in Western culture. Philosopher Robert Heilbroner has shown that "as late as the fourteenth or fifteenth century there was no land, at least in the modern sense of salable, rent-producing property."[14] The notion of private property which can be freely bought, exploited, developed, subdivided and sold is foundational to the contemporary market economy of capitalist countries. This is not just an economic concept. It is a fundamental way of seeing land.

The native peoples view land much differently than we do. Let's hear first how they understand us and our viewpoint. Chief Seathl of the Suwamish tribe wrote this to the President of the United States in 1855:

We know that the white man does not understand our ways. One portion of land is the same to him as the next, for he is a stranger who comes in the night and takes from the land whatever he needs.

The earth is not his brother but his enemy, and when he has conquered it, he moves on. . . . His appetite will devour the earth and leave behind only a desert.[15]

Native peoples throughout North America regard themselves as inseparable from the land. The land is something God has given them; they are to use it and be its custodians. The land is a friend. It must not be destroyed but passed on to their children and grandchildren. The land is security. As long as it is there they do not fear going without food and shelter. Moreover, the land is the source of identity and self-respect. They believe that if the land is destroyed or they are separated from it, they will die. This is why many of them view industrial expansion onto their lands as a form of cultural genocide.

Let's listen to how the Dene people describe their relation to the land:

Being an Indian means being able to understand and live with this world in a very special way. It means living with the land, with the animals, with the birds and fish, as though they were your sisters and brothers. It means saying the land is an old friend and an old friend your father knew, your grandfather knew, indeed your people always have known. . . . To the Indian people our land is really our life. Without our land we cannot—we could no longer exist as people. If our land is destroyed, we too are destroyed. If your people ever take our land you will be taking our life. [Richard Nerysoo]

The land is our blood. We were born and raised on it. We live and survive by it. [Joe Betsidea]

To us it is just like a mother that brought her children up. That's how we feel about this country. It is just like a mother to us. That's how serious it is that we think about the land around here. [Isodore Kochon][16]

Because the Dene world view entails an intimate and religious relation to the land, the notion of selling the land is foreign to them. You don't sell your mother, do you? Also, ownership is communal, not individual and private. Could one child make a special claim of owning her mother over against her sister? Of course not! The Dene and Inuit people share their material possessions and come to decisions on the basis of communal consensus, not democratic majority.

These contrasting views of land lead to contrasting approaches to land development. Native people are not against development per se. They simply approach it differently. The Dene themselves identify the two opposing approaches: one they call the "colonial" philosophy of development, the other the "community" philosophy. The colonial approach sees the north as the storehouse of resources for the industrial centers of the south. The Dene explain the consequences: "Oil, gas, and minerals move south to these centres. The profits which they generate move south along with them. The north becomes a hinterland dependent on the south; it loses its resources and gets welfare in return."[17] Colonial development, say the Dene, would have a terrible impact on the culture of the north. It would suck its resources dry, destroy the environment and kill the native way of life.

Is there any alternative? The Dene say yes! They propose a community approach to development whereby they might be granted legal ownership of land to which they have an aboriginal claim. They would own it communally and develop it on the basis of communal consensus. "Only community ownership of the land, land which has belonged to our people for thousands of years, can give us the ability to determine and follow our own way."[18]

The Dene people are committed to developing the land as custodians, not masters; as grateful recipients of divine blessing, not as greedy profit seekers. They have said they would even allow a pipeline to be built, with all of the risk that such a project brings to their way of life, if they were convinced that the oil would go to the aid of the poor in the Third World. They will not accept such a risk, however, if it is only to fuel the industrial machine of Canada or the United States.[19]

We have here two ways of life, two views of the land, two approaches to development, a culture within a culture. Whether these two world views can coexist within one society will be known through the passage of time.

While it is easy to speak of world views abstractly, we have tried to show that they are more than systems reducible to theoretical description. World views have spiritually formative and cultural power in the lives of individual people bathing babies and walking on the land. A merely theoretical description cannot convey their life-directing character. But having said all this, we want now to take a look at the theoretical explanation of world views, without reducing them to mere abstractions.

CHAPTER 2

Analyzing World Views

Humans are creatures of vision. This does not mean simply that we have eyes. Animals have eyes. Rather, it means that we are creatures who live our lives in terms of our perspective, our vision of life. Animals need no such perspective, for they are guided by instincts. Humans make life choices, and they make them in terms of their way of looking at things.

Consider the biblical notion of a "walk of life." The Scriptures tell us to walk by the Spirit and not by the flesh (Gal 5:25). Paul does not mean that we should leave our bodies behind, attempting somehow to be bodiless spirits. No, Paul is saying that the orientation of our walk of life, our direction, should be one of obedience to God, not disobedience.[1] We are to set our eyes and our vision one way and not another. This gets to the heart of what a world view is.

World View, World View: Everyone's Got a World View

A world view is never merely a vision *of* life. It is always a vision *for* life as well.[2] Indeed, a vision of life, or world view, that does not actually lead a person or a people in a particular way of life is no world view at all. Our world view determines our values. It helps us interpret the world around us. It sorts out what is important from what is not, what is of highest value from what is least.

A world view, then, provides a model *of the world* which guides its adherents *in the world*. It stipulates how the world ought to be, and it thus advises how its adherents ought to conduct themselves in the world. In a sense, each world view comes equipped with an eschatology, a vision of the future, which guides and directs life. The contrasts among the guiding visions of the Japanese concern for national honor, the Canadian colonialistic view of the north as a frontier and the Dene community philosophy of development illustrate this point well. We see in them three cultures, three world views, three directions of life and three anticipations of the future.

It is important to note, however, that world views (just like cultures) never belong to just one individual. World views are always shared; they are communal. Indeed, true community is possible only when people are bound together by a common way of life rooted in a shared vision of life. As we saw in our glimpse of Japan, Canada and the Dene, when a whole society is dominated by a particular world view, a cultural pattern emerges. Arnold DeGraaff comments that "political activities, legal, economic activities, marriage, family and child rearing practices are all expressions of a confessionally led way of life. Thus, each culture presents a coherent, meaningful pattern that finds its unity in the dominant vision of life."[3]

All the different aspects of a culture, whether its artistic life, economic structures or child-rearing practices, arise out of and are directed by its world view (see figure 1). That is what makes these different aspects of a culture hang together. How we raise our children, what kind of health care we receive and how we engage in economic transactions are all of one piece precisely because they are all guided by the same spirit. If they are not, then we experience a kind of spiritual schizophrenia, in which one part of life is led by one spirit and another part by a different spirit. Such a condition cannot go on indefinitely

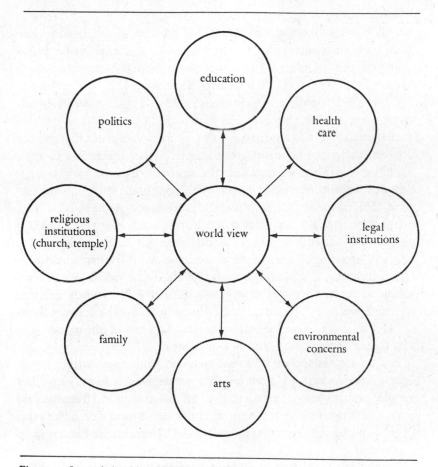

Figure 1.   Interrelationship of world view and culture.

without causing problems.

Cultural life, however, is not only *rooted* in the dominant world view; it also *orients* life in terms of that world view. This is why the arrows in the diagram point both ways. If a culture's vision of life leads to certain child-rearing, educational and economic practices, then those practices will themselves socialize the children to live in terms of that vision.

34 THE TRANSFORMING VISION

Worlds Apart

World views are intensely spiritual. They are a religious phenomenon. Hendrik Hart observes that "when you speak of the spirit of a movement you speak of its life, of its way of going about things, of that which truly makes it what it is."[4] We speak of the "spirit of the age" when one spirit or world view has a predominant role in a culture over a significant period of time.

Benjamin Whorf, a student of language theory, explains that the gap between different language groups reflects the differences in their world views. He hypothesizes that "the structure of the language one habitually uses influences the manner in which one understands his environment. The picture of the universe shifts from tongue to tongue."[5]

While we would not want to claim that each language reflects a unique and unified world view, nevertheless our language does affect our way of seeing. For example, there is no word for "wilderness" in Dene. It comes as no surprise then that the Dene world view has no wilderness but rather sees all land as a mother and friend. A different language means a different picture of the world. But the converse is no doubt true as well. Our language takes its shape out of our world view. The two reciprocally confirm one another.

James Sire has spoken of world views as "universes" within which people live.[6] Indeed, we often feel that we are worlds apart from other people, or that someone seems to live in a different world from us. And often that is precisely the case. Another person's world view *is* like a different world or universe, and its constitutive elements are like a map to that world.

This is why it is often so difficult for people of different visions of life to communicate and understand each other. They really are in different worlds, and they cannot penetrate each other's universe. Perhaps this accounts for the white man's failure to educate native children. The children don't know what the teacher is talking about because they are in a different "universe of discourse."

The Basis of a World View

So language reflects world view, and world view shapes language.

Where then does this cycle begin? What comes first, determining both world view and its verbal formulation? We would suggest that world views are founded on ultimate faith commitments.

Faith is an essential part of human life. Humans are confessing, believing and trusting creatures. And where we place our faith determines the world view which we will adopt.[7] Put another way, our ultimate faith commitment sets the contours of our world view. It shapes our vision for a way of life. People who doubt their world view are restless and feel they have no ground to stand on. They are often in the throes of a psychological crisis. But that emotional crisis is fundamentally religious because our world view rests on a faith commitment.

What is a faith commitment? It is the way we answer four basic questions facing everyone:[8] (1) *Who am I?* Or, what is the nature, task and purpose of human beings? (2) *Where am I?* Or, what is the nature of the world and universe I live in? (3) *What's wrong?* Or, what is the basic problem or obstacle that keeps me from attaining fulfillment? In other words, how do I understand evil? And (4) *What is the remedy?* Or, how is it possible to overcome this hindrance to my fulfillment? In other words, how do I find salvation?

When we've answered these questions, that is, when our faith is settled, then we begin to see reality in some sensible pattern. Out of our faith proceeds a world view, without which human life simply cannot go on.

The life of every person presupposes answers to these basic faith questions, but such answers are rarely held consciously. Though they can be brought to consciousness and made cognitively explicit, these questions and answers are not theoretical in nature. In other words, we base all our theoretical thinking on the pretheoretical answers we assign to the four ultimate questions.[9] (Chapter eleven will explain this idea further.) It would be a mistake to confuse a world view with a philosophical or theological system. A world view is always foundational to such a system, but it is never exhausted in it.

Let's articulate now the world views of the Japanese, North American and Dene, drawing their assumed beliefs from the way they live to answer the four ultimate questions: Who am I? Where am I? What's wrong? What's the remedy? Keep in mind that few people in any of these cultures would articulate their world view in this way, or have ever even thought about it. But, we would suggest, these unthought visions direct their lives nonetheless.

Japan: I am a member of the national family of Japan, direct descendants of the sun-goddess. I live in the land of the Rising Sun in harmony and oneness with the flow of nature. Disharmony occurs when I bring dishonor to my family or country. My task in life is to enhance the name of my national family, because true blessing only occurs when the superiority of Japan over the world of nations comes to pass.

North America: I am me, an individual, the free and independent master of my own destiny. I stand in a world full of natural potential, and my task is to utilize that potential to economic good. While I am hindered in this task by ignorance of nature and lack of tools for controlling it, nevertheless my hope rests in the good life of progress wherein nature yields its bounty for human benefit. Only then will all find happiness in a life of material affluence, with no needs and no dependence.

Dene: I am a Dene, a red man, placed here, a child of the land. The land is my mother; she gives me my life. The land is a gift that I respect, that I use with thankfulness and with which I live in harmony. But then the white man came, stealing my land, dispersing my people and cutting us off from the Great Spirit. Our salvation as a people is in rejecting the white man's ways and returning to our ancient traditions. Only then will the land be preserved and maintained for our children and grandchildren.

Evaluating a World View

How do we judge a world view? What criteria can we use? If, for some reason, it was necessary for us to choose a world view, what would compel us to select one over another? Our presentation of three world views has unavoidably presupposed certain judgments on them. Although we have tried to be fair, our discussion has most favored the Dene way of life and least favored the North American. The reason for this bias is that, although we are not Dene, the Dene world view seems on some points closer to our own than either the Japanese or North American visions of life.

Is this the only basis for judgment? Not at all. But it would be dishonest to discount how much we tend to be drawn to world views that coincide with our own or that offer insights which deepen our own vision. There are, however, other criteria by which a world view ought to be judged. But even these criteria are world view dependent. That is inescapable.

Reality. The primary criterion is simply this: does the world view in question accomplish what a world view ought to accomplish? As a vision of life, does it elucidate all of life? Can it open up all of life to those who adhere to it? Is it truly a *world* view? Or does it tend to open up only some aspects of life, ignoring others? Does it overemphasize or idolize one thing at the expense of another? For example, does the North American view of life, with its concern for development, overemphasize economic growth to the detriment of ecological responsibility? Does the Japanese emphasis on the group and loyalty result in a devaluation of individuals and their needs?

The fact is that God's creation coheres. Everything has its rightful place. And a world view that absolutizes either the economic side of life or group membership will inevitably do injustice to the coherence of the creation. Such injustice will become evident in certain breakdowns in the life of a culture. For example, an ecological crisis or psychological problems may point to a fundamental problem in a culture's vision of life. Eventually we will suffer the consequences of an idolatrous world view.

A world view that does not integrate and elucidate God's creation as it really is cannot lead to an integral and whole way of life.[10] The question is really whether our world view is consistent with reality. If it is not, then reality will fight against our misconstrued vision, urging us to change our perspective and our way of life.

A second question to ask is whether our perspective sensitizes or desensitizes us to issues of love and justice. Does it in effect legitimate all kinds of evil? Do we become blind to the selfishness and injustice that our own particular culture propagates, or can we still see it? If everything in our environment tends to legitimate our way of life, never challenging it, then perhaps we need a new prescription for our worldview glasses.[11]

Internal coherence. A world view should not only open up the creation to us, but it should also be internally coherent. A world view is not a set of beliefs arbitrarily thrown together; it should be a coherent vision of life. The issue is not so much a matter of logical coherence, but of unity of commitment. Does this vision of life hang together, or is it a house divided against itself?

The history of Japan in the last twenty-five years exhibits a world view that lacks internal coherence. The Japanese world view emphasized both a oneness with nature and the superiority of the Japanese over all other peoples of the world. The latter concern with group pride and loyalty was the religious driving force behind the postwar industrialization of Japan. But industrialization brought pollution, and pollution goes against the Shinto reverence for nature. Consequently Japan faces a world view crisis wherein one of its elements militates against another.[12]

Openness. The Bible suggests a summary question by which we can evaluate a world view (Deut 30:15-20): Does this view bring life or death, blessing or curse? In other words, does it open life up or close it down? In any respect that another world view brings life, we should all learn from it and allow it to correct our world view. For example, we have much to learn about gratitude from the Japanese and about land from the Dene.

We have implicitly suggested here an attribute of a "good" world view: it recognizes its own finitude and limitations. It is open to learn from other visions of life. This can be a difficult proposition. People hold to a world view because they assume it gives a better account of reality than any other. But a world view is not infallible and therefore it must not be absolutized. We dare not let our world view become fixed. It must be informed constantly by reality and, if we are Christian, by an increasing understanding of revelation, the Word of God.

This brings us back to the question of pluralism, which was introduced in chapter one. If one world view comes to cultural dominance, it must leave room for other visions to compete within that society. If it does not, we have reason to suspect its viability as a world view. Such a vision, totalitarian in character, has become an ideology.[13] We must recognize that our vision of life is always limited. It must always be open to correction and refinement, even from other world views.[14]

A Christian World View
Perhaps you are wondering how a Christian world view could possibly be corrected. After all, isn't it rooted in our faith in Jesus Christ, who is the Way, the Truth and the Life? Yes, it is. But if we did an empirical study we would discover that there are many Christian world views.[15] Unfortunately, as we will see in chapter six, Christians often hold a world view at variance with their confession of Christ.

At issue here is the internal coherence of our world view. Is it consistent with its faith commitment? If it is not, then it lacks integrity. It is often just such a realization that precipitates a world view crisis for many Christians. One day we come to realize that our world view is not the world view of the Scriptures; we see that it is not consistent with our confession that Jesus is Lord. Then we need either to deny our confession and look elsewhere, or to begin to overhaul our basic way of looking at life and living it.

For Christians, the ultimate criterion by which we judge our world view is the Bible. It is God's revelation of reality. Paul tells Timothy that the Scriptures have a purpose; they are to teach, reprove and correct us, and to train us in righteousness so that we may be equipped for a life of good work (2 Tim 3:16-17). If we seek a world view that leads to life and not death, then we must go to the Scriptures for instruction. And as our world view is informed, corrected and shaped by the Scriptures under the guidance of the Spirit, we will receive direction for our way of life. The next three chapters will investigate that biblical world view, the pathway for our walk with God.

PART 2

The Biblical World View

CHAPTER 3

Based on Creation

"In the beginning God created the heavens and the earth." With this majestic proclamation the Bible opens. And so does the biblical world view.

As Christians we often pay only lip service to the biblical doctrine of creation. We think it is important perhaps for refuting evolution, but otherwise we do not place much value on it. Instead, we focus on Christ and the message of salvation.

Yet the world view of the Scriptures does not begin with Christ and salvation. It begins with God and creation. The first article of the Apostles' Creed emphasizes the Genesis account: "I believe in God, the Father Almighty, Maker of heaven and earth." This is where Christianity begins. Creation is the biblical starting point.[1]

Jesus Christ and the redemption he brings are undoubtedly the focus of the Scriptures. The biblical message is a call from sin to reconciliation with God. But what is sin? And what do words like *salvation, redemption* and *reconciliation* mean? It is impossible to offer an answer to these questions if we do not have an implicit idea of creation. For it is creation that is affected by both sin and salvation.

To talk about sin we must look at how God's creatures disobeyed him and how his good creation was distorted. What is salvation but the outworking of God's love for his creation as he restores it from the bondage and effects of sin? Creation, then, although certainly not the central message of Scripture, is the underlying foundation. Indeed, without an understanding of the biblical view of creation our understanding of both sin and redemption will inevitably be distorted. In world-view terms, we cannot answer the questions "What's wrong?" and "What's the remedy?" unless we first address the issues of who we are and where we are. Answering the four world view questions will direct us through the biblical themes of creation, fall into sin and redemption in Christ. These themes constitute the basic flow and movement of the Bible.

We must remember, however, that these are not merely interesting ideas to be discussed. A world view is always incarnated. The world view of the Scriptures, coming with God's authority, calls his people to commitment and action. Just as we cannot be neutral about the person of Christ and the salvation he offers, so we cannot ignore the radical implications of the biblical teaching on creation.

By Word, By Wisdom

Much can be said about creation but let us begin by noting two significant images that the Bible uses to portray God's creation of the world.[2] The first occurs in Genesis 1, where God creates by uttering commands. The second image comes from Proverbs 8. There wisdom is the craftsman through whom God made the world.

These two images, creation by the word and creation by wisdom, have long intrigued Christians. But what do they convey? And how do they contribute to our understanding of the biblical world view?

Look first at the image of creation by the word. After the majestic opening statement which proclaims God's creation of the entire universe, the earth is described as formless and empty, like a dark, brooding ocean. And "the Spirit of God was hovering over the waters" (Gen 1:2). The scene is one of preparation. Something momentous is about to happen. Then "God said, 'Let there be light,' and there was light" (Gen 1:3). This picture of God's command and creation's response becomes the paradigm, or model, for the rest of the chapter. Eight times God brings new creatures to life out of his original, unformed creation by his commanding word.[3]

The impact of this image makes us aware of the power and sovereignty of the Creator. His authority is such that he needs only to speak and creation obeys. By his sovereign decree he gives order and structure to the world. As Isaiah 55:10-11 says, God's word does not return to him empty. It always accomplishes his will. In this case, God's word accomplishes creation.[4] Hence the recurring refrain in Genesis 1, "and it was so."[5]

But another important refrain occurs in Genesis 1: God is pleased with the order and complexity of the world he has made. The incredible variety of creation—day and night; sky, land and sea; sun, moon and stars; fish, birds, animals and human beings—all this, in the simple yet profound language of Genesis 1, is declared *good*. Why? What pleases God?

It is good, first of all, that the world exists in all its diversity, with so many kinds of creatures. God is pleased with the many different things he has made. Why? Because it is an expression of his will. Creation constitutes a pattern of obedient response to his commanding word. This is what God judges to be good.

As if to fix in our minds just how pleased God is with his world, Genesis 1 affirms the goodness of creation no fewer than seven times. And the final affirmation, at the end of the chapter (v. 31) states emphatically that "God saw all that he had made, and it was very good."[6]

The idea of creation by God's word, however, is by no means limited to Genesis 1. The psalms, for instance, also speak in this way. They are full of praise to God for his creation. A classic example is Psalm 33:6-9:

By the word of [Yahweh] were the heavens made,
    their starry host by the breath of his mouth.
He gathers the waters of the sea into jars;
    he puts the deep into storehouses.
Let all the earth fear [Yahweh];

let all the people of the world revere him.
  For he spoke, and it came to be;
  he commanded, and it stood firm.[7]
Another example is Psalm 148:5-6, which calls on God's creatures to praise him:
  for he commanded and they were created.
  He set them in place for ever and ever;
  he gave a decree that will never pass away.
These two passages clearly echo Genesis 1. They portray God as the sovereign Creator who gives the orders; his world, the creation, exists in response. Creation is by God's word.[8]

But creation is also by God's wisdom. Notice Proverbs 8, where wisdom, personified in the feminine form, explains her relationship to both God and creation.

  [Yahweh] possessed me at the beginning of his work,
    before his deeds of old;
  I was appointed from eternity,
    from the beginning, before the world began.
  When there were no oceans, I was given birth,
    When there were no springs abounding with water;
  before the mountains were settled in place,
    before the hills, I was given birth,
  before he made the earth or its fields
    or any of the dust of the world. (8:22-26)

In the beginning, before creation, God possessed wisdom. Indeed, God is wise. But he also appointed and gave birth to wisdom. What does this mean? It means the wise Creator came up with a brilliant plan. He gave birth to wisdom; his incredible scheme was conceived. And he designated this wise plan as the model for the world he created. Wisdom was there before the world was made, and yet she was also there *at* creation and actually had a part in it.

  I was there when he set the heavens in place,
    when he marked out the horizon on the face of the deep,
  when he established the clouds above
    and fixed securely the fountains of the deep,

when he gave the sea its boundary
    so the waters would not overstep his command,
and when he marked out the foundations of the earth.
    Then I was the craftsman at his side.
I was filled with delight day after day,
    rejoicing always in his presence,
    rejoicing in his whole world
    and delighting in mankind. (8:27-31)

So wisdom is not merely God's plan for creation in the abstract; it is the wise way he actually designed and ordered the world. The picture is of the Creator crafting and structuring the creation with skill, measuring out the ocean, setting bounds, marking the horizon, fixing the heavens and clouds in their places. In all this, wisdom is God's "craftsman."

The image of creation by wisdom is found elsewhere in the Bible. For example, in Job 28:25-27 God's method of creation is described much as it is in Proverbs 8.

When he established the force of the wind
    and measured out the waters,
when he made a decree for the rain
    and a path for the thunderstorm,
then he looked at wisdom and appraised it;
    he confirmed it and tested it.

And we could turn to Proverbs 3:19-20, which declares:

By wisdom [Yahweh] laid the earth's foundations,
    by understanding he set the heavens in place;
by his knowledge the deeps were divided,
    and the clouds let drop the dew.

To the ancient Hebrew mind, terms like *wisdom, understanding* and *knowledge* are almost synonymous. They refer to the same basic reality, the wise way God has designed and structured creation.

The wise and marvelous way God has made the world is cause for great rejoicing. His creation is good! We have wisdom in Proverbs 8 dancing for joy before the face of God, delighting in his works. And the psalmist exclaims in what is perhaps the most beautiful creation psalm in the Bible,

How many are your works, O [Yahweh]!
  In wisdom you made them all;
  the earth is full of your creatures. (Ps 104:24)
David, reflecting on his own creatureliness, offers a personal account
of this awareness when he says to the Lord:
  I praise you because I am fearfully and wonderfully made;
    your works are wonderful,
    I know that full well. (Ps 139:14)
These selections are a mere sampling of the biblical writers' awareness
of the wonder and goodness of creation, an awareness that spills over
into praise of the Creator.

Worthy of Worship

Both the creation-by-wisdom and the creation-by-the-word passages
occur in a context of praise and worship of God. Creation is never discussed in an abstract, speculative manner in the Scriptures. Instead, the
focus is on God as the wise and all-powerful Creator. Whether for
his keen insight in the amazing design of the world or for his commanding authority to which creation responds, God is worthy to be praised.

A passage that combines these two emphases and focuses on the Lord
as the only One worthy of worship can be found in Jeremiah 10:1-16.
It is a classic biblical diatribe against idols, which, in contrast to Yahweh,
are both impotent and stupid. These false gods have no part in creation.

But God made the earth by his power;
  he founded the world by his wisdom
  and stretched out the heavens by his understanding.
When he [utters his voice], the waters in the heavens roar;
  he makes clouds rise from the ends of the earth. (Jer 10:12-13)[9]
This passage combines creation by wisdom and by the word. And both
are cause to praise the Creator.

There is another link between the creation-by-the-word and creation-
by-wisdom passages. Both are dominated by terms that refer to the way
God gives form and measure to the world through the act of creation.
We could compare, for example, two of the longest passages we have
mentioned. In Genesis 1, the Creator's word orders and structures the

unformed earth; in Proverbs 8 wisdom is God's "craftsman" by whom creation is given limit, measure and bounds.

This theme of the structuring of creation is found in all the passages we have mentioned and in practically every other biblical reference to creation. The basic idea, in the words of Isaiah 45:18, is that God "fashioned and made the earth, he founded it; he did not create it to be empty, but formed it to be inhabited." The allusion here is to Genesis 1:2, the picture of the desolate, empty earth. But this was not the final state of creation. Far from being a chaotic wasteland,[10] the completed world is a cosmos, an orderly, inhabitable universe structured by the wise commands of God himself.

A number of the terms used in these creation passages connote more than just order or structure. They imply a *stable* order, a *dependable* structure; God's word is faithful, founding and establishing the world, fixing it firmly in place.[11] This emphasis points to the radically dependent nature of creation. In ourselves we have no structure or existence. We are but flesh and dust, here today and gone tomorrow. Isaiah 40: 6-8 compares us to grass or flowers. "The grass withers and the flowers fall, but the word of our God stands forever" (v. 8). Creatures are, by definition, totally dependent. We exist only because God's wise word sustains and preserves our being. The psalmist, in 119:89-91, affirms this when he says:

Your word, O [Yahweh], is eternal;
   it stands firm in the heavens.
Your faithfulness continues through all generations;
   you established the earth, and it endures.
Your laws endure to this day,
   for all things serve you.

A Covenant with Creation

Contrary to the deistic idea of creation, God didn't just "speak" in the beginning and then leave the world to its own devices.[12] Creation is not a clock God wound up and left to run by itself. To this day he still speaks; his voice echoes throughout all creation. This is the only reason the world is still here. Creation is essentially constituted as a *response* to the laws of God. We do not initiate our own existence. Instead, we exist because God's word—his decree, his commands and his laws—stand forever. We can depend on the Creator because he is faithful to his word.

To put this another way: God is faithful to his covenant. We usually think of God's covenant as his relationship with Abraham or Israel, or of the new covenant through Jesus. But the underlying reality behind these historical covenants is God's relationship with creation itself. This is made explicit in the book of Jeremiah, where Yahweh, speaking through the prophet, issues a challenge: "If you can break my covenant with the day and my covenant with the night, so that day and night no longer come at their appointed time, then my covenant with David my servant —and my covenant with the Levites who are priests ministering before me—can be broken and David will no longer have a descendant to reign on his throne. . . . If I have not established my covenant with day and night and the fixed laws of heaven and earth, then I will reject the descendants of Jacob and David my servant" (Jer 33:20-21, 25-26).

In other words, God's relationship with day and night, heaven and earth, is as much a covenant as is his relationship with his people. And this covenant is linked explicitly with the fixed regularities of creation which God established and appointed. Creation is a covenantal response to God's word. Just as the Torah, or Law, was given to Israel in the context of a covenant relationship, so God's laws and ordinances for all creation are covenantal. The entire universe is intimately related and bound to Yahweh, and he lovingly cares for his world.[13]

This covenantal bond between God and creation, this model of God's sovereign and loving relationship to the world, corresponds to the biblical theme of the kingdom of God. God is the great King over creation, and he rules his subjects by sovereign decree. He gives his law, and creation responds in obedience. He governs the world by his wise word.

The kingship of Yahweh is proclaimed throughout the Bible and in many places is directly linked to creation. Psalm 95:3-5, for example, calls us to sing for joy:

For [Yahweh] is the great God,

the great King above all gods.
In his hand are the depths of the earth,
and the mountain peaks belong to him.
The sea is his, for he made it,
and his hands formed the dry land.

God is thus the Creator-King. And his rule is bound to his preserving and sustaining of the world. As Psalm 96:9-10 declares:

Worship [Yahweh] in the splendor of his holiness;
tremble before him, all the earth.
Say among the nations, "[Yahweh] reigns."
The world is firmly established, it cannot be moved.

Because God rules the world, creation can depend on him for its continuance. Because he is faithful to his covenant, because his sovereign and wise commands stand firm, the earth is firmly established.

If we were to pull together the various strands of biblical thought and imagery we have been exploring, we would see a unified picture: beginning with the images of creation by God's word and wisdom, we have integrated these seminal ideas with the wider biblical view of the world as God's good kingdom, the realm of his wise and sovereign rule. All creation (which includes us as human creatures) is covenantally bound to God and is constituted essentially as a response to his laws. The entire universe is dependent on Yahweh for its being, and he is praised and worshiped by his creatures. In the familiar words of Psalm 19:1, "The heavens declare the glory of God; the skies proclaim the work of his hands." They declare his glory because they are an obedient expression of his will. Psalm 148:8 even mentions "stormy winds that do his bidding" (literally, "that fulfill his word"). And so the psalmist in 119:91 declares to God, "All things serve you."

In this intensely religious model of reality, this model of God's intimate relationship to the world, we find the biblical answer to the world view question "Where am I?" Our answer provides the foundation on which the edifice of the total biblical world view is built. All the major categories and themes of Scripture are understood in terms of this underlying foundation. The nature of sin and redemption, for example, are always viewed in the context of God's covenant and kingdom. And,

as we shall see later, this foundation is particularly important for understanding the new covenant inaugurated by Jesus—which he usually
called the kingdom of God.

But this foundation is also important for understanding who we are
as human beings.

In God's Image

What does it mean to be human? Who are we as human beings? These
questions have haunted the religious and philosophical thinkers of all
civilizations, including our own, and many different answers have been
offered. Yet these questions are not subjects for the philosophical elite
only. They are world view questions, basic to everyone, that concern
our vision of life. All of us adopt, consciously or unconsciously, some
idea of what it means to be human. And we live by this idea. We may not
be able to articulate what we believe ourselves to be, but we function
with an implicit awareness of an identity, a vision of who we are as human beings.

Who does the Bible say we are? Its initial answer is that we are God's
creatures, living in his kingdom, dependent on his wise and loving rule.
Just like the heavens that declare his glory and the winds that do his
bidding, we are servants of Yahweh, the Creator-King. This is intrinsic
to our creaturehood.

Yet we are different from the heavens and the winds, as well as from
the plants and the animals, and we sense this difference. We are God's
servants, but the nature of our service is unique. It is encapsulated in
the biblical term *the image of God,* introduced in Genesis 1:26-28.

> Then God said, "Let us make man in our image, in our likeness, and
> let them rule over the fish of the sea and the birds of the air, over the
> livestock, over all the earth, and over all the creatures that move along
> the ground." So God created man in his own image, in the image of
> God he created him; male and female he created them. God blessed
> them and said to them, "Be fruitful and increase in number; fill the
> earth and subdue it. Rule over the fish of the sea and the birds of the
> air and over every living creature that moves on the ground."

The meaning of this formulation—"image of God"—has been the subject of much debate over the centuries.[14] The image has usually been linked to some feature, or constellation of features, thought to be shared by God and humanity, which distinguishes us from animals. Some thought it our rational capacity, others our moral nature, our spirituality or our personhood. This approach to the meaning of the image as something structural, or static, may be called the "wide" sense of the term. A relational, dynamic approach in which the image refers to the level of a person's morality, or the degree of conformity to the perfect character of God, may be called the "narrow" sense of the image. The first refers to our humanity per se; the second sees the image as normative, the standard to which we are to conform. Many people have tried to combine these two emphases.

There is a serious problem here, however. Many interpretations of the image have been influenced more by non-Christian philosophy than by the Scriptures themselves. This need not be the case. We would be the first to take issue with a naive biblicism, with the idea that we can approach the Bible *tabula rasa,* as if we were not influenced by any prior extrabiblical ideas and assumptions (in this case, ideas regarding what it means to be human). Yet the Scriptures are themselves the proper source of our understanding of what it means to be in God's image. And their central teaching is quite clear when each portion is read in context.

Our creation in the image of God is related to two important biblical notions: our dominion or rule over the earth, and the religious choice of serving God or idols.[15] These two notions, which correspond somewhat to the wide and narrow senses of the image, are in reality intertwined, but it will be useful to distinguish them as we look at what it means to be human.

Ruling over the Earth

The ideas of the image of God and our rule of the earth occur near each other in the Genesis narrative, making their connection seem natural. But this is by no means their only link. Throughout Genesis 1, God is portrayed as the Creator-Lord who rules his world by sovereign decree. Then, with the creation of mankind, the idea of the image of God is introduced. Almost in the same breath God blesses his special creatures and gives them dominion over the earth. He gives them a royal authority and a realm to subdue and rule.

We see in Genesis 1 an intended analogy between the limited authority over the earth that humans enjoy and the ultimate sovereignty of Yahweh. The former is portrayed as a reflection or likeness of the latter. We are created, male and female, in the image of the sovereign Lord. As Psalm 8 emphasizes, we have been crowned with glory and honor, and made rulers over God's creation.

But let us be more precise. How exactly do we image God? In what does our rule consist? What does it mean to subdue the earth? We find an initial answer to these questions in the next chapter of Genesis. Unlike the panoramic sweep of Genesis 1, which presents mankind as the climax and crown of God's drama in creation, Genesis 2 focuses specifically on God's human creatures. Instead of merely appearing in the last act, so to speak, we consistently hold center stage; our unique nature and task are clarified. Specifically, we are told that God planted a garden in Eden and placed Adam in it "to work it and take care of it." Perhaps the Revised Standard Version is better known. There Adam's task in the garden is "to till it and keep it." Whatever the translation, the point is the same. The twofold original human task is to *develop* and *preserve* our creational environment.

We are, first of all, to "work" or "till" the garden. Or, in the words of the New American Standard Bible, we are to "cultivate" the garden. This last translation helps us understand the passage better because of the explicit link between the words *cultivate* and *culture*. Culture is the result of cultivation. A bacterial culture, for example, is a colony of organisms intentionally reared and tended for some purpose. Both *culture* and *cultivate* refer essentially to our human interactions with the world.

Culture, of course, embraces a great deal. Anything to which we put our hand (or mind) changes—we cause some sort of development. Although development and change may take place without human agency (for example, growth processes or natural disasters), human interaction with or cultivation of our world always constitutes culture.

Culture and history are therefore inseparable, almost by definition. Culture refers to what human beings *have developed,* so culture is essentially historical. The fabric of human life is developmental; this is intrinsic to our nature as human creatures. Yet this is also true of God's nonhuman creation. Because some sort of development is always taking place, the world may be said to have its own history independent of human culture-forming. But uniquely *human* history, the historical development of mankind, is based on our constant interaction with and cultivation of reality as we find it.

This interaction with reality, our human culture-forming, is intrinsically a communal or social phenomenon. Its social character is suggested by the mention in Genesis 1:28 of both man and woman as the image of God. It is also indicated quite clearly by the precise command God gave them. Their task was to subdue or rule the earth. But because Adam and Eve are only two, God tells them to be fruitful and increase and fill the earth. How could they otherwise subdue it? The cultural development of the pristine, undeveloped creation is thus not conceived as a task for an individual. Culture is based solidly on society. Our humanity, in the image of God, is essentially a cohumanity. We are sociocultural beings, called by God to work together in developing and cultivating the creation.

Besides gardens, we also cultivate relationships, manners and forms of worship. We harness animals and the forces of nature. We formulate and develop ideas and traditions, and we construct not only technological objects but social groupings and institutions as well. All these activities and their results are cultural; that is, they are humanly developed realities. Culture refers not merely to intellectual and aesthetic pursuits (as in "high culture" or a "cultured" person). Culture covers the whole range of human society. It includes not merely art, music and scholarship, but also such things as our economic and political life, religion, the church, education, technology, the media, marriage, family life, advertising and entertainment. To be a cultural being is, quite simply, to be human.[16]

So the primal command to subdue the earth (often called the creation mandate) is a cultural mandate. In all our cultural activities and affairs—that is, in all human actions, artifacts, relationships and institutions by which we interact with and develop creation—human beings provide evidence of their God-given rule of the earth. The image of God, in its central reference to the idea of subduing the earth, designates humans as cultural-historical beings.

We can see here one major emphasis of the biblical vision of life: wholeness. As we have begun to answer the world view question "Where am I?" we have seen the goodness of God's varied creation affirmed by the biblical writers. And now, in our discussion of "Who am I?" we see that human beings are recognized in the Scriptures as full-orbed cultural creatures, called by the Creator to go forth and develop the earth. This wholistic approach is both refreshing and life affirming. The biblical world view connects with reality. It affirms our humanness and rings true to what is there.

Checking Our Interpretation

Yet are we interpreting the Scriptures correctly? Could our view of the cultural nature of humanity be merely a modern interpretation, foreign to the actual mandate in Genesis? Perhaps we are reading a contemporary notion into an ancient text. In response, let us note two key points: the literary structure of the book of Genesis, and the examples of cultural development recorded in Genesis 2:4—4:26.

First, a strange refrain occurring periodically in Genesis provides us with an interpretive clue: "These are the generations of . . . " "Generations" is an attempt to translate the Hebrew term *toledoth*. The refrain "These are the *toledoth* of . . . " divides the book at eleven places. This refrain signals the literary structure of Genesis; each instance serves as a preface or title for the section of either narrative or genealogy that follows.[17]

Sometimes the *toledoth* refrain introduces a section containing little more than a genealogical list.[18] In those cases, *toledoth* literally means "generations" or "offspring." But in about half of the refrains the meaning is much broader.[19] An instructive example is Genesis 2:4, which reads, "These are the generations of the heavens and of the earth when they were created" (KJV). Coming right after the creation of the heavens and the earth, this heading introduces their "generations," in the sense of what was "generated" from them.

Although there is still a genealogical element here, a reading of the section which follows (2:5—4:26) would suggest that the meaning is actually much closer to the idea of historical development. The *toledoth* refrains therefore support our interpretation of the creation mandate. In fact, they incorporate this emphasis on development and history in the very structure of the book of Genesis.

The second key point is that the *toledoth* of the heavens and the earth records a series of examples of cultural development and innovation. The initial creation narrative tells how man and woman are issued the mandate to subdue the earth. The following section on the relevant "generations" or historical developments explicitly mentions how they responded to that mandate.

Adam's primitive culture in Genesis 2, for example, includes not only gardening (agriculture) but marital relations (Adam and Eve), the beginnings of language (the naming of the animals) and even the first poem (Adam's two couplets in praise of Eve). A second group of examples, found in Genesis 4:20-22, gives even stronger support. Here we find accounts of three makers of history, the originators of three traditions: Jabal, "the father of those who live in tents and raise livestock"; Jubal, "the father of all who play the harp and flute"; and Tubal-Cain, "who forged all kinds of tools out of bronze and iron." Human beings are clearly recognized in the early chapters of Genesis as cultural beings, and now their historical development is noted explicitly.

The implication is that creation has a built-in eschatology. The biblical world view is not only wholistic but also dynamic. Creation is going somewhere. Sin's introduction into the world is not equivalent to the beginning of change, as some world views suggest. Change would have come anyway. Creation was meant to be developed. It underwent development even before humankind came on the scene. God himself changed (by development) his original creation into the varied world we now inhabit. In the image of the Creator, we are called on to exercise our rule in developing the earth. We are to cultivate the creation garden.

What happens when a garden is cultivated? The answer is in the last two chapters of the Bible. There, in the *new* heavens and earth (the creation redeemed from the crippling effects of sin), we find a contrast to Genesis 2. Instead of a garden as in Genesis (obviously reflecting a primitive situation), we find in Revelation a full-fledged city.

This eschatological movement from the garden to the city was intended by God. True, the Fall has occurred in the meantime; sin has entered the picture. Nevertheless, the vision of Revelation 21 and 22 portrays a world purified from the Fall and its effects. And development remains a part of the purified world.

The cultural mandate is part of God's original plan for the world. Salvation does not negate it but rather fulfills it. It is intrinsic to human nature to be culture formers. Human beings have the God-given mandate to develop the creation.

Preserving the Earth

The Bible does not, however, support unbridled development. The twofold task given Adam was to develop and to *take care of,* or *preserve,* the garden. The intent of the biblical mandate is quite distinct from the modern Western vision of human conquest and exploitation of nature. (This latter idea is the root of the colonial view of "land as frontier" which we discussed in chapter one and which we'll pick up again in chapter eight.)

We may note here that the conquest motif is a thoroughly secular view, quite foreign to the spirit of the Scriptures. In the Bible the non-human world is not viewed as something "out there." We do not stand over-against God's other creatures. Instead our solidarity with creation is affirmed. The mountains and the trees are God's servants too! We are in a covenant relationship with the world, a relationship of husbandry.

While we reject any pantheistic notion of revering nature, we should also recognize the crucial element of loving care and preservation in the biblical mandate to subdue the earth. We are to till *and* keep the garden. Our culture forming is not to be done selfishly but with real care for the creation. To be faithful to the image of God, our cultural development of the earth is to be good, wise and loving—like Yahweh's covenental rule.

To be human therefore means two basic things. First, we are creatures of God. And like all creatures we live only in response to God's loving word. We are not autonomous. This is quite distinct from the world view of Western culture, which regards humanity as a law *(nomos)* unto itself *(autos)*. But far from positing our own standard, we are in fact subject to the law of God. We are his servants, living under his rule. This is intrinsic to our creaturehood. Second, human beings are unique. We are cultural-historical creatures. God has placed us in a position of authority over the earth to cultivate and develop it. Both servanthood and authority are central to our humanness. Herein is the initial biblical answer to the world view question "Who are we?"

This answer is well illustrated in Jesus' parable of the talents in Matthew 25:14-30. The master in the parable went on a journey and put his slaves in charge of his finances (the talents), to invest them wisely during his absence. In the same way God rested from his work of creation and gave humans the authority to develop his possessions, which are the creation he has entrusted to us.[20] But accountability matters, for the master returns and judges his slaves for the way they used his possessions. So it is with us. We may not simply rule the earth as we please, because we do not own our kingdom. Our authority is derived from God, and thus it takes on the character of stewardship.

The financial analogy in the parable is quite significant. The root of the English word "economics" is the Greek *oikonomos,* the common New Testament word for a householder or steward, one entrusted to oversee and administer his or her master's property. This is in direct contrast to the modern view of economics, which views each person as an autonomous agent, subject to no external restraints in his or her exploitation of the world.

The biblical idea of stewardship, however, balances authority with servanthood. This strikes at the heart of our humanity. Although we are indeed lords of the earth, we are also servants of God. We are called to exercise our rule in obedient response to Yahweh's ultimate sovereignty. Subduing the earth is an issue of covenantal responsibility.

CHAPTER 4

Acknowledging the Fall

It is our covenantal responsibility to serve the Lord our Maker, and yet we are not forced to do so. It is possible to disobey, to depart from who we are called to be. And this possibility became reality in the Fall. The Christian world view answers the third basic question, "What's wrong?" in terms of human disobedience to God.

Human beings are inherently religious creatures. We cannot live without a god, even if it is one of our own making. We need a center, an ultimate focus, a point of orientation for our lives. We have in fact two alternatives. Either we serve the Lord and obey his will, or we practice idolatry in disobedience. These are the spiritual antitheses, the either/or of life which the Bible repeatedly addresses. In all our doings, in all our ordinary human and cultural activities, we constantly face these two covenantal ways.

The issue of spiritual antitheses can help us grasp what the Bible means by the image of God. Although the underlying principle of the image of God is our nature as cultural beings, mandated to rule the earth in Yahweh's stead, the overriding biblical orientation to the term is explicitly post-Fall. That is, the full meaning of the image of God takes into account human disobedience, particularly idolatry.

How can this be? What is the relation between our creation in the image of God and the covenantal choice of serving God or idols? The answer lies in the precise nature of idolatry, a practice that doesn't concern most Christians today but which is mentioned often in Scripture. In light of this frequency, an analysis of idolatry is essential to our understanding of what it means to be created in God's image.

Idols: Usurping God's Place

Let's begin with Paul's discussion of sin in the first chapter of Romans. According to Paul, we live in God's world and are intuitively aware that there is a powerful Creator worthy of our worship. But we suppress this knowledge. Human beings down through the ages have rejected God's revelation of himself through creation. They have not acknowledged or worshiped him as God. Instead, they "exchanged the glory of the immortal God for images made to look like mortal man and birds and animals and reptiles. . . . They exchanged the truth of God for a lie, and worshiped and served created things rather than the Creator—who is forever praised" (Rom 1:23, 25).

There are only two basic categories: the Creator and the created. If we do not worship God, we will focus on something in creation and elevate it to the status of divinity. We will worship a *false* god. Our intrinsically religious nature will never allow us *not* to worship. Either we pledge ultimate allegiance to Yahweh, the only true God, or we commit ourselves to some created thing and make a god out of it. We must choose one or the other, for we cannot live without a god, and we cannot have two—at least not for long.

Jesus said it is impossible to serve two masters. One will have to give way to the other because worship is an exclusive practice. For this reason Paul talks about idolatry as an exchange: it is something we do *instead* of serving God. Yet Yahweh alone is worthy of worship. Created things are not worthy, for they are only his servants, dependent on his rule for their existence. Idolatry is essentially a declaration of autonomy and independence from our Creator, our rejection of his rightful kingship.

The consequences can be terrible. If we do not worship the King of creation, if we reject his rule, then we will disobey his laws. That is why the prophets brought a twofold message of judgment to Israel: the people have forsaken Yahweh for idols, *and* the land is full of lawlessness and injustice. Idols are at the root of disobedience.

No wonder, then, that idolatry is denounced at the start of the Decalog, or that Paul in Romans 1 saw idolatry as the beginning of human disobedience! If our allegiance is not to God, we have no reason to keep his standards. So idolatry is portrayed in the Bible not as merely one sin among many, but as the epitome of sin. It is the central act of disobedience which disrupts Yahweh's rule over human life.

But there is more. Idolatry involves *idols*. Although the essence of idolatry is the rejection of God's kingship and the attempt to worship something in creation, idolatry in ancient times was carried even further. People tried to *represent* God (or what the worshiper thought was god) by means of a carved or cast statue. Idolaters constructed a visual image of the deity to be worshiped.

But notice that this practice is not recorded in the early chapters of Genesis. There, human sin and rebellion against God are clearly noted, but no reference is made to literal, physical idols. References do not appear until the time of the patriarchs.[1] It would be unwise to try to date the beginning of idolatry from this evidence alone, but notice a second intriguing fact. This same prepatriarchal section of Genesis that makes no mention of idols is the only part of the Old Testament to refer to human beings as the image of God. A startling observation. Apart from four references to humanity in God's image in the early chapters of Genesis (1:26-27; 5:1; 9:6), the Old Testament is silent on this topic. Why? Could these early references to our creation in God's image be connected with the *lack* of early references to idolatry?

A connection is indeed suggested by the fact that the Bible uses the term *image* to refer to both human beings and idols. The same Hebrew word is used.[2] But more important than the word itself is the underlying idea. What does it mean for an idol to be an image, particularly the image of a god?

Idols: Usurping Our Place

In the ancient world an idol was not thought to be an actual god. It was not naively identified with the deity it was supposed to represent. Instead, the idol was viewed as the local means by which the deity became present to people. It was the visible embodiment of the god, representing his or her power and majesty. As an image the idol was symbolic; it mediated and manifested the god's glory and rule to those around.[3]

This understanding of what it means to image a god coincides with our earlier interpretation of the image of God in man. Just as the idol was supposed to be the visible, local manifestation of the god, the means by which he or she became present, so human beings are supposed in Genesis to represent Yahweh on earth. His Spirit and power accompany them, and he exercises his rule over the earth through them. The essential link between the image of God and the cultural mandate is thus confirmed. Human beings are God's ambassadors, his representatives, to the rest of creation. We are the stewards he has set in authority over the earth to manifest his presence and to reflect his glory in all our cultural doings.

But note that the image consists in our *bodily* representation of God. The whole person, and not some inner spiritual part, is created in God's image. We reflect God's glory and represent him on earth by our total, physical presence. Indeed, visibility is of the essence, for we are to make the invisible God visible by our lives. In the whole range of our cultural activities we are to demonstrate Yahweh's loving rule.[4]

Idolatry is wrong, therefore, not because it tries to make God visible (which is precisely the human task) but because it goes about this task in the wrong way. Instead of accepting and fulfilling our created responsibility to represent the Lord in the whole range of our cultural activities, we project this responsibility onto idols. We therefore deny our calling to live in such a way that God's loving rule can be seen, and we begin to cultivate the earth in disobedience. Idolatry is thus the illegitimate alternative to the genuine human task to image God. It is equivalent to living a life so distorted by false worship that it ceases to reflect God's standards.

Idolatry, then, has two distinct, though related, qualities. It involves not only false worship but, by extension, false imaging. Both are warned against in the Ten Commandments. Hear what God says in Exodus 20: 3-5:

1. You shall have no other gods before me.
2. You shall not make for yourself an [image] in the form of anything in heaven above or on the earth beneath or in the waters below. You shall not bow down to them or worship them.[5]

There is an important distinction between these two commandments. The first focuses on Yahweh as the only true God; the second focuses on humankind as the only true image of God. It is not our prerogative to arbitrarily invent whatever it is we want to worship, for there is only one God. Similarly, we do not have the authority to designate what the image of God is going to be. God settled that when he created us. And he says to his human creatures, *You* image me! Not idols. Idols are simply not adequate representations of Yahweh. That task is reserved for human beings.

Idolatry thus usurps not only God's proper place but ours too. It contradicts both God's rightful kingship as Lord of the universe and our fundamental human calling to represent him in daily, cultural obedience —to image him in our lives.

The relationship of idolatry to our creation in God's image indicates, therefore, our intrinsically religious nature, the either/or structure of our life. As human beings we constantly stand before two paths: one leading to the true worship of Yahweh, the other leading to the service of idols. Either we image God in our loving rule of the earth, or we forfeit that task in disobedience.

Choose You This Day

Human beings must then choose between two covenantal ways, the two possible responses to God's laws for our life. We cannot *not* respond. We live only in covenant relation to our Maker. We exist only in response to his sovereign rule.

Just as we cannot be neutral in relation to him, so he is not neutral toward us. God judges our response to his laws. The covenant, in other words, has sanctions.

The book of Deuteronomy is particularily instructive here. Deuteronomy is the Bible's only complete text of a covenant renewal ceremony. It documents what took place between Yahweh and Israel on the plains of Moab before the people entered the Promised Land.

The climax of the book and the classic summary of the covenant comes in Deuteronomy 30:15-20. Although these verses occur in the context of a specific historical covenant between Yahweh and Israel, they are based on the creation covenant and present the same basic structure.[6] The passage begins with Moses laying out before the people the two covenantal ways. "See," he says, "I set before you today life and prosperity, death and destruction." He describes the first way:

> I command you today to love [Yahweh] your God, to walk in his ways, and to keep his commands, decrees and laws; then you will live and increase, and [Yahweh] your God will bless you in the land you are entering to possess.

Then he turns to the second way:

> But if your heart turns away and you are not obedient, and if you are drawn away to bow down to other gods and worship them, I declare to you this day that you will certainly be destroyed. You will not live long in the land you are crossing the Jordan to enter and possess.

Bringing his address to a climax, Moses then says:

> This day I call heaven and earth as witnesses against you that I have set before you life and death, blessings and curses. Now choose life, so that you and your children may live and that you may love [Yahweh] your God, listen to his voice, and hold fast to him. For [Yahweh] is your life, and he will give you many years in the land he swore to give to your fathers, Abraham, Isaac and Jacob.

What we have in the book of Deuteronomy, focused in this passage, is a picture of Yahweh, the great King, the sovereign Lord, giving his laws, his instructions for right living, and calling his people to unswerving, total commitment and obedience. The two covenantal options of loving obedience or idolatrous disobedience are laid before them.

The consequences are clear. God responds to *our* response. The way of obedience is the way of shalom; it results in life and blessing from the hand of God. But the way of disobedience is the way of death and the judgment curse.

The consequences are inevitable. For disobedience goes against the very grain of creation itself. Sin is rebellion against both the structure and the Structurer of reality. Such rebellion is inevitably self-defeating and self-destroying.

In contrast, to fulfill one's created nature, to be in obedient harmony with God's laws, is the fullness of life. Hence we find in the carefully structured format of Genesis 1 a repeated pronouncement by God that creation's original response to his word was good, even very good. And mankind at creation receives the covenant blessing (1:28).

In Genesis 3, however, the opposite is true. There, in the account of the Fall, we find that the result of human disobedience is the pronouncement of a series of curses (3:14-18). Or, as Paul explains in Romans 6:23, "the wages of sin is death." That is the only result possible when we disobey the word of life.

The Bible elsewhere calls these two ultimate directions of life the ways of wisdom and of folly. Just as God's wonderful design for creation shows his wisdom (evident in his wise laws for all of life), so our obedient response to these laws constitutes *our* wisdom. To rebel against God's creational standards is regarded in the Scriptures as the utmost folly.

A Sacred/Secular Split?

The paths of wisdom-obedience and folly-disobedience cut across everything we do. We are called to serve the Lord and acknowledge his kingship in the whole range of our cultural activities. There are no sacred/secular compartments here. Our service to God is not something we do *alongside* our ordinary human life. The Bible knows no such dichotomy. In the biblical world view all of life, in all of its dimensions, is constituted as religion. From our economic choices to our recreation, from our prayer life to the way in which we bathe our babies, in every

cultural action and deed, we live only in response to the cosmic, creation law of God. This is God's universe throughout. And we are called
to be responsible respondents to his overarching Torah.

But the sacred/secular split dies hard. Many object, arguing that
God has standards for some human actions but that to others he is simply indifferent. They argue that life indeed is religious in some sense
but that it cannot strictly be identified with religion. After all, our Christianity does not apply directly to *everything* we do. It does not apply,
for example, to such "secular" activities as agriculture and art.

Or does it? Hear what the Bible says in Isaiah 28:

When a farmer plows for planting, does he plow continually?
    Does he keep on breaking up and harrowing the soil?
When he has leveled the surface,
    does he not sow caraway and scatter cummin?
Does he not plant wheat in its place,
    barley in its plot,
    and spelt in its field? (Is 28: 24-25)

How does the farmer know how to plow the fields and sow the seeds?
"His God instructs him and teaches him the right way" (v. 26). The passage continues:

Caraway is not threshed with a sledge,
    nor is a cartwheel rolled over cummin;
caraway is beaten out with a rod,
    and cummin with a stick.
Grain must be ground to make bread;
    so one does not go on threshing it forever.
Though he drives the wheels of his threshing cart over it,
    his horses do not grind it. (vv. 27-28)

All this about such a mundane activity as a farmer's threshing methods!
How does he know the right way to thresh grain? "All this also comes
from [Yahweh] Almighty, wonderful in counsel and magnificent in
wisdom" (v. 29).

In other words, the farmer's understanding of the right way to farm
—the practice of good agriculture—is regarded in the Bible as coming
from God. The farmer is in touch with God's wisdom. He has discerned

and is following God's wise laws, his creational norms, in this sup-
posedly secular area of life.

Take another biblical example, this time regarding the building of
the tabernacle (Ex 31). God explains to Moses that he has chosen a master
craftsman named Bezalel to oversee work on the tabernacle. The significant point here is the reason given for Bezalel's expertise. The Lord says:
"I have filled him with the Spirit of God, with skill, ability and knowledge in all kinds of crafts—to make artistic designs for work in gold,
silver and bronze, to cut and set stones, to work in wood, and to engage
in all kinds of craftsmanship" (Ex 31:3-5).

This passage can shatter our preconceptions about what it means to
serve God; it may shatter our world view. Exodus 31 can cause a gestalt
shift in the way we see the relevance of Christianity to life. It tells God's
purpose in our being filled with the Spirit of God.

The Spirit of God enables us to live obediently, to live a holy life in
accordance with his standards. God filled Bezalel with his Spirit so that
he would be led into "artistic obedience." Yahweh, the Creator and
Lord of the universe, the one who created us artistic beings, wanted a
good job done on his tabernacle. So he enabled Bezalel to discern and
obey his creational standards for craftsmanship and art.

These two examples from Isaiah and Exodus illustrate the central biblical teaching: *all* we do is to be done from a heart filled with love for
God. If our lives are not an expression of our love for him, they will express rebellion against him. That is simply our religious nature as God's
image bearers. All our cultural life is subject to Yahweh's norms, and
we are called to respond to him in obedience.

Clashing Kingdoms

We have, however, fallen short of our calling. We are broken people
who have served idols rather than reflected the image of God. We live in
a creation fallen and groaning for redemption. Sin is not simply a
created possibility; it is a present fact. This is our common human experience. The Fall has occurred, and the curse has been proclaimed.

But how did this come about? How did sin enter God's good creation? Satan attempted to take over the creation by inciting its inhabi-

tants, subjects of Yahweh, to treason against their rightful Ruler. He led a rebellion against the lawful King of creation and set up his own renegade kingdom, called in Colossians 1:13 the dominion of darkness. Satan styled himself a ruler (the Scriptures call him a prince) although he is only a pretender to the throne, having no rightful claim to authority.[7] His kingdom, established in direct opposition to God, is parasitic. Since Satan has no legitimate realm (or creation) of his own to rule, he lives off God's rule. His dominion consists of attempts to distort God's good creation. His kingdom of destruction works *against* God's good and wise order for creation.

Thus Satan led humankind into covenant disobedience. He tempted humankind to reject the rule of Yahweh and to issue their "declaration of independence" from their Creator. The consequences are devastating. When communion with the Creator of life is broken, death inevitably results. Life is no longer whole but broken. Personal, interpersonal and social breakdowns abound because life is severed from its source. Moreover, the declaration of independence proves to be an illusion. Rather than finding autonomy, we find that we are still servants—bound to a despot who rules over a kingdom of slaves.

Yet the Fall affected more than humanity. Our sin has enslaved the earth. Because God had given us a unique authority over creation, our disobedience brought the entire creation under a curse. Henceforth the cultural task, human life in all its aspects, is a struggle. By ceasing to image God in our rule of the earth, we go against the grain of life; we contradict the way things were meant to be. Indeed, we contradict our very personhood. No longer do we care for creation; in fact, we begin to experience the earth as an enemy. Instead of preserving and developing creation, we destroy and exploit it. We rule the earth in disobedience. Like the despotic usurper, we act like despots (Jn 8:41-44).

As a result, "the whole creation," says Paul in Romans 8:19-23, is groaning and waiting for the time when it will be "liberated from its bondage to decay and brought into the glorious freedom of the children of God." The creation is waiting, in other words, for *our* liberation. Only then will it be truly restored. Because it was enslaved by our sinful rule (the curse that was the consequence of our disobedience), only our redemption will guarantee its freedom.

Two kingdoms are at war. A spiritual battle is going on, a clash of the kingdoms which permeates the entire range of human activities. Just as the two covenantal ways cut through all that we do, so do the two kingdoms. Just as all our cultural life is *created* and thus under God's rule, and as we are called to serve him in all that we do, so all our life is now *fallen*. There is nothing in creation that sin has not touched: "The whole world is under the control of the evil one" (1 Jn 5:19).

Although God still calls us to obediently execute our cultural task, the usurper bids us to pledge allegiance to his renegade kingdom and so deny our true calling. The insightful words of C. S. Lewis cut to the heart of our post-Fall situation: "There is no neutral ground in the universe: every square inch, every split second, is claimed by God and counterclaimed by Satan."[8]

CHAPTER 5

Transformed by Redemption

The biblical world view affirms the goodness of creation and speaks of . the human task in lofty terms. But it does not romanticize life. It is utterly realistic about the human predicament. In fact, if the biblical world view were to stop with the question of what's wrong, we would have cause for deep despair.

The biblical vision, however, offers hope. It not only addresses the problem of evil, but it tells us how God has answered the fourth world view question, "What's the remedy?"

Redemptive History
The Bible promises that Satan's illegitimate claims will one day cease; his kingdom will be destroyed. Genesis 3, the very chapter recording the Fall, announces the first clue of God's redemptive plan. In the midst of his declaration of judgment on sin, God tells Satan:

I will put enmity
    between you and the woman,
    and between your offspring and hers;
he will crush your head,
    and you will strike his heel. (Gen 3:15)

Here, embedded in the covenant curses, comes a promise of an end to these curses: through the offspring of the woman, says God, Satan will be vanquished.

The offspring of the woman is, of course, Jesus, the promised Messiah, the One who came to destroy forever the kingdom of darkness and to effect God's redemption of the fallen world. But the "offspring" also refers to the descendants of Adam and Eve who lead up to Jesus. Although God ultimately brings salvation through Jesus, he ushers in Jesus through a long historical process that we may properly call redemptive history.[1] This is the story the Scriptures tell. They recount the drama of God's mighty acts in history—leading up to his greatest act, the Incarnation of Christ—through which he reverses the Fall, counters sin, and so restores and redeems his fallen creation.

Any world view built on the Bible must, as a result, focus on Christ's incarnation—his life, death and resurrection. But we need also to understand something of the history of redemption, all that preceded and set the context for his coming. While Jesus is at the center of God's redemptive plan, God did not send him immediately to the scene of the Fall—prepackaged, so to speak. Instead, the God of history prepared the world for the coming of the Messiah.

Redemptive history, as the Bible recounts it, proceeds primarily through a series of historical covenants which God established with mankind. The way God relates to us in salvation thus builds on his original, fundamental relationship with creation itself. Redemption, like creation, is intrinsically covenantal. Hence at the climax of redemptive history we have the new covenant inaugurated by Jesus and sealed in his blood.

But to understand more clearly the significance of that climactic covenant, let us look first at two Old Testament covenants, those which God made with Noah and with Abraham. We will see how they contrast both with each other and with the new covenant.[2]

The covenant with Noah. According to Genesis, Adam's initial disobedience led to further and worse disobedience. Genesis 6:5 says that "every inclination of the thoughts of [man's] heart was only evil all the time." Our fallen state could hardly be described more intensely. The book of Genesis tells us that God got so sick of these disobedient creatures of his, these creatures who had ceased to reflect his image, that he was grieved he had ever made them. And so judgment came—the flood.

But this was still not final judgment. For God had promised hope through the offspring of the woman. So he saved Noah and his family. Here we find the parting of the two covenantal ways. The whole earth was locked into disobedience and rebellion against God, yet "Noah was a righteous man, blameless among the people of his time, and he walked with God" (Gen 6:9). We see two ways of life with two sets of consequences. Disobedience brings a curse—in this case, the flood. But obedience brings a blessing.

After the flood God established his covenant with Noah and all his descendants and with every living creature. He promised that he would never again bring a judgment of this kind on the earth, no matter how evil people became.

Although this is the first covenant in the Bible actually *called* a covenant (see Gen 6:18), it is clearly built on God's foundational covenant relation with his creation. Six times in Genesis 9:9-17 God explicitly says that the Noahic covenant is with "every living creation" or with the earth itself. Important elements found in Genesis 1, such as our creation in God's image (9:6) and the mandate to be fruitful and fill the earth (9:1, 7), are repeated. Even the regular covenantal pattern of creation is mentioned in 8:22:

As long as the earth endures,
seedtime and harvest,
cold and heat,
summer and winter,
day and night
will never cease.

Yet this is definitely not God's initial covenant with creation. Sin has happened in the meantime. Certain modifications take into account the post-Fall situation, like the warning against taking human life in 9:5-6.

This is God's *redemptive* covenant. Here God is at work, not creating the world or sustaining its existence, but working out his plan of salvation, his plan to redeem his fallen world. And he begins by narrowing the earthly population to one righteous family, even though the covenant remains universal in scope.

The covenant with Abraham. A new, significant stage in the history of redemption is marked by Genesis 12. Until this point God's covenant of redemption, established with Noah, has been creation-wide—between God and the whole earth. From Genesis 12 to the end of the Old Testament, God's original covenant with creation still stands (hence the world is still here). Yet God establishes a special covenant with Abram (later called Abraham) and his descendants.

Out of all the world, God is now specially related to one family, soon to become one nation. God promises to make a great people of Abraham's descendants and to give them the land of Canaan as their inheritance. And the purpose is that "all peoples on earth will be blessed" (Gen 12:3). God, as King of the covenant, gives Abraham his word of law, his covenant requirement to "walk before me and be blameless" (Gen 17:1). Yet what is dominant through all the phases of the Abrahamic covenant is his word of *promise* (Gen 12:1-9; 13:14-17; 15:1-21; 17:1-21). The emphasis is on God's faithfulness to the covenant and what he will accomplish through Abraham and his descendants.

Just as the Noahic covenant was with all people and all creation, so later in the new covenant through Jesus Christ it would once more be open to all. But for the time being, Yahweh narrows the focus of his redemptive action, and thus his redemptive covenant, to Abraham and his descendants. This is the basic focus of the covenant in the rest of the Old Testament.[3]

Why did God limit his covenant in this way? What was the purpose in excluding all but one people and nation, even temporarily?

In Scripture, people and land are closely intertwined. "Who we are" (God's culture-forming image bearers) is inseparable from "where we are" (in God's good creation which is to be tilled and kept). God's original intent at creation was for an obedient, holy people who would reflect his image and live in covenant relationship with him in an as yet undefiled land. But then sin came, affecting both humanity and the earth. It then became God's plan to create a *new* holy people (the redeemed body of Christ), who would live before him in covenant relationship in a *renewed* land. Second Peter 3:13 mentions "a new heaven and a new earth, the home of righteousness."

But to accomplish this the Messiah had to come, the One whose task it would be to destroy sin at its root, thereby freeing creation from its bondage to the evil one. To do this God focused his covenant temporarily. He first created a provisional holy people, Israel, living in a provisionally purified land, Canaan. In the midst of *these* people, in *this* land, the Messiah was born and grew up. Although God did bring a partial redemption through his covenant with Abraham and his descendants, the main purpose was to prepare a context into which the Messiah would come, the One who would inaugurate the new covenant and thus effect the total and complete redemption of creation.[4]

The Nazareth Manifesto

The term *new covenant* first appears in Jeremiah 31:31-34, where it speaks of the Messianic age. We see it later, specifically in connection with Jesus, in 1 Corinthians 11:25 and Hebrews 8:6-13 and 9:15. But the references are few and far between. Only the Corinthian passage refers to Jesus' use of the term. But another term, practically equivalent to the idea of the new covenant, was always on his lips, expressing the sum and core of his message. That term is *kingdom of God.*

The idea of the Messianic kingdom is central to the synoptic Gospels, and we know from the biblical record that Jesus started his public ministry by announcing the coming of this kingdom.[5] After his baptism in the Jordan River and his temptation in the wilderness, Jesus returned to Galilee. There in his home province he proclaimed the gospel of God (Mk 1:14). What was the nature of this gospel, this good news? "The time is fulfilled, and the kingdom of God is at hand; repent and believe in the gospel" (Mk 1:15 NASB). In Jesus' teaching, the gospel of repentance and faith was integrally tied up with the coming of the kingdom of God.

The Gospel of Luke, unlike Mark (and Matthew 4:17), does not *begin* the account of Jesus' ministry with his proclamation of the kingdom. Why does he omit this if the idea is so central to Jesus' preaching? The most likely explanation is that Theophilus, the man Luke addressed (1:3), was a Greek and would not have grasped the full meaning of this Hebraic idea. He would not have been sufficiently acquainted with the biblical world view to understand what Jesus meant by the kingdom of God. So, instead of using this image at the start, Luke records for us an incident in which Jesus *explains* the nature of the kingdom of God— without actually mentioning the term.

We learn in Luke 4 that, after his baptism and temptation, Jesus returned to his hometown of Nazareth and went to the synagogue on the sabbath. The scroll of the prophet Isaiah was handed to him. He opened it at chapter 61. What follows could well be called the Nazareth Manifesto, for it outlines how Jesus saw his mission. He read to the people:

The Spirit of the Lord is on me,
  because he has anointed me
  to preach good news to the poor.
He has sent me to proclaim freedom for the prisoners
  and recovery of sight for the blind,
to release the oppressed,
  to proclaim the year of the Lord's favor. (Lk 4:18-19)

Then he handed back the scroll, sat down (as was the custom of the rabbis when they were going to teach) and proclaimed: "Today this scripture is fulfilled in your hearing" (Lk 4:21).

Jesus had quoted an Old Testament prophecy of the Messianic age.[6] But what did it refer to? Was the Messiah's mission restricted to a purely "spiritual" sphere, the way these verses are often interpreted? Or does the passage really mean the literal, concrete things it says? Follow what happens a few chapters later, in Luke 7.

Jesus has been performing miraculous works, and the news has reached John the Baptist, who is in prison. So John sends two of his disciples to Jesus with the question, "Are you the one who was to come, or should we expect someone else?" (Lk 7:19). Jesus answers quite simply, "Go back and report to John what you have seen and heard:

The blind receive sight, the lame walk, those who have leprosy are cured, the deaf hear, the dead are raised, and *the good news is preached to the poor"* (v. 22).

In other words, Jesus says that the evidence of his Messiahship could be found in the physical works he was performing. The words in italics are fulfillments of Isaiah's prophecy which Jesus previously quoted in his manifesto. Luke portrays Jesus' ministry as the fulfillment of a Messianic prophecy. It was twofold in nature: the verbal proclamation of the good news of God's kingdom plus the physical manifestation of the kingdom.

Kingdom and Covenant

But why should we call this the kingdom of God? What does the good news have to do with God's kingship or rule? Just this: God's kingship is covenantal in nature. We saw in chapter four that God binds his creatures to himself by his sovereign word; he rules by decree. Creation, as God's covenantal kingdom, thus responds to his word in either obedience or disobedience. The significance of the Fall is that humankind gave allegiance to another king, resulting in covenantal disobedience to God's laws. So we experience not only intentional human sin and various kinds of interhuman bondage, but also bodily disease and death. In all these ways God's good creation has been distorted by the Fall.

Into this context came Jesus as Messiah and Savior. He came to restore creational obedience to God. This restoration consisted first and foremost in the forgiveness of sins, but it also involved the total restoration of human lives (including the healing of diseases) through the work of Christ.[7] By engaging in this ministry of restoration, Jesus, while on earth, demonstrated the good news he proclaimed—that God's redemptive rule over creation had begun. The kingdom of God had arrived.

Although the kingdom of God is the central designation of God's redemptive rule in the synoptic Gospels, the term is not common in other New Testament writings. Yet the restorative nature and cosmic scope of salvation are constant ideas in the entire New Testament world view. Several passages from Acts, Revelation and the Epistles confirm this.

We have already noted Paul's statement in Romans 8:19-23 that all creation is groaning under the curse of futility, awaiting the day when it will be released from its bondage following the liberating redemption of the children of God. We find the same notion of the re-creation of the entire universe in 2 Peter 3:10-13 and Revelation 21:1. Both refer to the passing away of the old and the coming into being of "a new heaven and a new earth." Acts 3:21 records a similar thought, speaking of a future time when, in accordance with his promise through the prophets, God will "restore everything." And Colossians 1:20 proclaims in parallel fashion that God's plan is to "reconcile to himself all things, whether things on earth or things in heaven" through the atoning blood of Christ. We could compare this reconciling work with God's eternal purpose as stated in Ephesians 1:10, "to bring all things in heaven and on earth together under one head, even Christ."

All of these passages emphasize two themes. In the first place, *all* things (in heaven and on earth) are to be redeemed. Redemption is truly cosmic in scope. This theme accords entirely with the wholistic nature of our covenantal life discussed in the last chapter. No area of creation is beyond God's reach or his care. No aspect of our cultural life is exempt from his redemptive plan and righteous rule.

The second point is that these passages (with the exception of Ephesians 1:10) view salvation as *redoing* something. Romans 8, for example, describes redemption as buying back from slavery and, as a consequence, setting free. Colossians 1 speaks of reconciliation, which means bringing back into unity and harmony those who were separated by enmity. And 2 Peter and Revelation both clearly emphasize re-creation, the restoration of the original, creational goodness lost by sin.[8]

God's plan of salvation thus involves the entire universe. The new birth is not limited to humanity alone. The passage in John's Gospel where we find the phrase "born again" contains the only references in that Gospel to the kingdom of God (3:3-5). God loves the *world,* and therefore he renews it (gives it a new birth) and tells Nicodemus to be part of this renewal through his own new birth.

The Usurper Bound
But what about Jesus' part in this? How did he actually bring about the

kingdom of God? How is the Messianic kingdom based on the work of the Messiah? To answer these questions we turn to an incident which relates the coming of God's kingdom to the death-resurrection triumph of Jesus. (This incident is recorded in all three synoptics: Matthew 12: 28-29, Mark 3:27 and Luke 11:20-22.)

Jesus has been accused of casting out demons by the power of Satan. In reply he points out that if this were the case, Satan would be working against himself. "But if I drive out demons by the finger of God, then the kingdom of God has come to you" (Lk 11:20). Then comes the key analogy: "No one can enter a strong man's house and carry off his possessions unless he first ties up the strong man. Then he can rob his house" (Mk 3:27). Jesus is saying that his coming to earth had a specific purpose. It was to attack and overpower Satan, the strong man, and to tie him up. This is what Christ accomplished by his death and resurrection. Having overpowered and bound the strong man he was now in a position to reclaim the possessions which the pretender prince had taken from God.[9]

The victory of God's kingdom, however, required the death of Jesus Christ as the Lamb of God, who suffered the covenant curse for our sins. The full covenantal judgment of God for all the sins of the world fell on Jesus as he hung on the cross, forsaken by his Father. Because he suffered that abandonment, we are no longer cursed for our disobedience. Jesus became the final, ultimate sacrifice for sin, and by his death and triumphal resurrection we are offered the free covenant blessing of abundant and eternal life in fellowship with God. The work is all God's. We have merely to repent of our sins and turn to Christ in faith.

Through Jesus' death-resurrection victory he inaugurated the kingdom of God. He began to restore the obedience of God's once-rebellious subjects. The Messianic kingdom that Jesus brought is thus the reversal of evil, the renewal of God's good creation.

Yet Jesus did not attempt to establish the kingdom totally and immediately, while he was on earth. He did not, for example, set out to heal every sick person in the world. That was not his task. He came to inaugurate the kingdom. By his words and works he announced the inbreaking of this kingdom; his miracles pointed to the fact that God had begun to undo the work of Satan.

The kingdom of God, explained Jesus, is like a little leaven put into a lump of dough, which then permeates the entire lump (Mt 13:33 and Lk 13:20-21). The point of this parable, however, is not that the kingdom will grow gradually until it fills all things. Jesus was not a postmillennialist.[10] He did not believe that the world would get better and better. He recognized that the growth of the kingdom was a struggle and a battle. But the parable encourages us. Just as the leaven of sin has radically permeated all of creation, so also does the leaven of the kingdom now reach "as far as the curse is found." And in the final days the kingdom will come in its fullness by the cataclysmic intervention of God himself.

We still have in creation both the leaven of the kingdom and the leaven of sin.[11] Hence the significance of Christ's first and second comings: the kingdom comes in two phases. While his first coming signified his inauguration of God's kingdom, his second will herald its consummation. First is D-day, Christ's first advent when he struck the decisive blow to sin and Satan. Here the battle is already won; Satan's kingdom is doomed. But the war is not yet over. Skirmishes continue and the dominion of darkness fights on. Yet in principle the battle is won. And at the end will be V-day, victory day, when Christ returns to wipe out sin, annul the effects of the Fall and thus bring in our full redemption.[12] "Then the end will come," says Paul, "when he hands over the kingdom to God the Father after he has destroyed all dominion, authority and power. For he must reign until he has put all his enemies under his feet. The last enemy to be destroyed is death" (1 Cor 15:24-26).

Satan is totally defeated. The victory reverberates in Revelation 11:15: "The seventh angel sounded his trumpet, and there were loud voices in heaven, which said: 'The kingdom of the world has become the kingdom of our Lord and of his Christ, and he will reign for ever and ever.' "

God's victory in the end will be so complete that the kingdom is described as a stone, cut without hands, which grows into a mountain and fills the entire earth (Dan 2:34-35, 44). The coming kingdom of God is so radical in its purifying and transforming effect that nothing (and no *kind* of thing) escapes its influence. Nothing in creation is in principle beyond the scope of redemption.[13]

Where do *we* stand in the midst of this cosmic redemption? How do we fit into God's plan of salvation? Who are we as redeemed humans? And what is our redemptive task? Here we turn for our answers to a prominent New Testament theme: the renewal of the image of God.

Renewal of the Image

We noted earlier how little reference the Old Testament makes to our creation in God's image, and we linked this fact to the presence of sin, particularly idolatry. The New Testament, in contrast, is full of such references. The emphasis, however, is not simply on our creation in God's image but on the restoration of this image in the church, the body of Christ, which is viewed as the new and redeemed humanity.

The very fact that the church, in whom the image of God is restored, is called the body of Christ, points us toward Christ, the head of the church. The New Testament refers to him as *the* image of God *par excellence* (Col 1:15; Heb 1:3; 2 Cor 4:4-6). Although these passages could be taken to refer to Christ's unique status as God, they also refer to his perfect humanity.[14] Christ is the perfect image of God, the paradigmatic man who completely represented God and mediated God's presence in the full range of his earthly, human life. Hence the classic statement in John 14:9, "Anyone who has seen me has seen the Father," could just as easily refer to Christ's humanity as his deity. In fact, the Gospel of John is full of statements concerning Christ's perfect obedience and oneness of purpose with the Father, an obedience and oneness we are called to imitate.

This teaching is found elsewhere in Scripture. For example, Paul views Christ as a second Adam. He fulfilled the imaging task that the failure of the first Adam had begun to erode. Romans 5:12-19 contrasts Adam and Christ. While Adam disobeyed God, bringing sin into the world and passing it on to all humanity, Christ by perfect obedience brought salvation, which he now gives to all who believe in him. And 1 Corinthians 15:49 adds encouragement. Just as Christians have borne the likeness of Adam, failing to image God in our lives, so we shall one day bear the likeness of Christ, imaging our Creator once more.

Scripture promises that on that final day, when Christ returns to consummate his kingdom, "we shall be like him" (1 Jn 3:2). In fact, says Paul, God has predestined the church "to be conformed to the likeness of his Son, that he might be the firstborn among many brothers" (Rom 8:29; see Heb 2:10-11). But this restoration of the image is not only intended for the future. It is also the present reality of our sanctification, our growth to maturity in Christ. Because Christ, the head of the church, is our standard and measure (Eph 4:13), our imaging task of reflecting God's rule in our lives is equivalent to our growing in likeness to Christ (Eph 4:13). Just as Christ fully represented God in all his earthly life, so we as the church and Christ's *body,* are to manifest visibly the life and presence of Christ our Lord, here and now.

The Spirit Who Renews

Christ is present in his church by the Holy Spirit who indwells us. Thus the church as Christ's body is an extension of Christ's presence on earth. He lives in us by his Spirit, who conforms us to his image. The Holy Spirit is therefore crucial to the New Testament understanding of our imaging task.

The coming of the Holy Spirit at Pentecost marked a significant new stage in redemptive history. His coming proclaimed that the age of the new covenant was here. Under the old covenant, God's Spirit is only occasionally mentioned, and then only in connection with certain select leaders in Israel. Under the new covenant the Spirit is poured out on all who believe (Acts 2:17-18, 38). Under the old covenant, God's redemptive dwelling was localized in the tabernacle and then the Temple. In the new covenant it is the people of God—Christ's body, as well as the body of each Christian—who are said to be the temple of the Holy Spirit. We are the spiritual house in which God dwells.[15]

The Spirit is also given as a pledge or guarantee of our future inheritance and glory (2 Cor 1:22; 5:5; Eph 1:13; 4:30). Because of God's abiding and transforming presence with us, we can be assured that we will share in this future kingdom, the cosmic redemption he will bring about.

By the Spirit we have a foretaste of the blessing of the future kingdom—our transformation into God's image. Just as Bezalel was filled with the Spirit so that he could discern and obey God's creational laws (chapter four), so the Spirit leads Christ's body today into full-orbed holiness. Hence Paul constantly prays for the church, that the Spirit would give them the wisdom to discern God's will and to live obediently in all they do (Eph 1:17; Col 1:9-10). We must not limit these spiritual-sounding prayers of Paul to some narrow area of life. Precisely because our spirituality consists in the renewal of our total life before God, we must live wisely, heeding the voice of God's Spirit in the entire range of our cultural life.[16] Thus we begin to conform to God's righteous rule.

Under the old covenant, when the Spirit was not universally given, God gave detailed covenantal laws to his people. They needed, in the words of Paul, a "schoolmaster" or "tutor" to lead them to Christ (see Gal 3:24). But now that Christ has inaugurated the new covenant, such detailed laws are conspicuously absent. God has not removed the standards for the whole of our lives (analogous to the scope of the Old Testament laws). He has rather given the Holy Spirit to the church to put us back in touch with God's creational standards. Now we may discern his will in all our endeavors. As God proclaims through Jeremiah, prophesying about the new covenant: "I will put my law in their minds and write it on their hearts. I will be their God, and they will be my people" (31:33).

How does this new covenant relate to the Bible, God's written Word? The Scriptures for us are a direction-setting book. The written Word of God is a living Word; it cuts to our hearts, corrects us and sets us on the right path (2 Tim 3:16-17; Heb 4:12). Yet the instructions for right living do not, by any stretch of the imagination, cover all the life situations we encounter. Instead, the law is written on our hearts by the indwelling Holy Spirit, and we are entrusted with the responsibility to interpret and apply this law in our lives.

Thank God we are not left to our own individual decisions! We have not only God's creational and written Word but also the Spirit of the living God, who sensitizes us to God's standards and prods us to obedience. Hence Paul's description of the Spirit's work under the new covenant in contrast to the old. He calls the new covenant "the ministry of the Spirit" that "brings righteousness" (2 Cor 3:8-9).

The old covenant had in itself brought only condemnation. Paul points out that the fading reflection of the *shekinah* glory on Moses' face at Mount Sinai does not compare with the glory of the Lord reflected by Christians. While Israel is still veiled to the Messianic message (and thus to the image), we are unveiled to and by the Spirit. "And we, who with unveiled faces all reflect the Lord's glory," says Paul, "are being transformed into his likeness with ever-increasing glory, which comes from the Lord, who is the Spirit" (2 Cor 3:18).

This transformation is meant to be taken quite literally. Our reflection of God's image is the transformation of our entire lifestyle. In Ephesians 4:24, Paul reminds us that we have put on "the new self, created to be like God in true righteousness and holiness"; in Colossians 3:10 he says this new self "is being renewed in knowledge in the image of its Creator." Terms like *righteousness, holiness* and *knowledge* are to be taken in their Hebraic sense, where they refer broadly to wholistic covenantal obedience.

Imaging God—Together

Not only do we have the help of the Holy Spirit to aid us in discerning and practicing God's will, but we also have each other. The church as the body of Christ has many members. It is a central teaching of the New Testament that Christianity is not individualistic. Paul always describes our individuality in terms of our unique contribution to the body (1 Cor 12:7-31). And when he tells us to be renewed in the image of Christ, he is never speaking merely to individuals but always to communities of believers (Eph 4:7-16, 22-24; 5:1-2; Col 3:5-17). Our task of understanding God's laws and imaging him by our obedient lifestyle is a communal task. We must struggle together in discerning how to respond as authentic Christians to the secular culture in which we live—this culture with its deeply ingrained, often distorting effects on human life.

But it is not easy to determine an obedient Christian response to culture. It's too easy to offer glib answers, and they will usually be wrong. God's people need to wrestle together, listening to what the Spirit says to the churches. There are many pressing issues: nuclear war, economic materialism, the computer explosion, a Christian academic witness, a Christian contribution to political and social healing, a Christian transformation of the arts and an enrichment of aesthetic life in general. Some issues seem more pressing than others, depending on our particular gifts and interests. And in many areas we do not have a long Christian tradition of reflection or action on which to draw. In some areas Christians have only recently begun to respond.

How difficult it is then to present an integrated, overall picture of a Christian response to culture! That is why this book on the Christian world view is a team effort, and not merely coauthored. We two have learned so much from dedicated Christians wrestling with their faith, the Scriptures and the world around us that it would be impossible to give a full catalog of our indebtedness.

Our point is that we cannot image God alone, if for no other reason than that the image has a reference to our cultural rule over creation. And, as we have already seen, human culture-forming is a communal task. The biblical motif of the body of Christ also leads us in this direction. As Christians acting in unity, we need to address the issues of our culture. It means starting right where we are, with the economic choices we make each day, with our jobs and our families. We need to begin developing a Christian perspective in our studies, and to wrestle seriously with how our Christian faith has affected and will affect both our choice of career and the way we carry out our work. We need to take seriously the cultural "bite" of what it means to be renewed in God's image. Through the gospel of Christ we have been reinstated as servant-lords of creation. The cultural mandate has been renewed: this is the meaning of the New Testament teaching that we shall rule with Christ.[17]

Nevertheless, our communal task as the church is not cultural development, pure and simple. We live in a fallen world—we are not in the pristine creation. By God's grace we have received the good news of his kingdom; we have submitted our hearts to the King and experienced his transforming love in our lives. Yet the culmination of the kingdom is still to come. The eschaton, the new heaven and the new earth, has not yet arrived. Christ redeems all things, but we do not yet see all things redeemed. We live between the times; the new age has begun, but the old age is still here. We are in neither the garden nor the New Jerusalem.

Christians in these "last days" are therefore called to engage in the imaging task as *ministers of reconciliation*. That is our redemptive task: it is the vocation of the body of Christ to work together in a fallen world, seeking to bring the forgiveness, healing and renewal of God's rule to bear on every area of life. Individuals need to repent, and cultural patterns need to be redirected. Obedience to Christ requires no less. That is the full and radical depth of the gospel.

So we are faced with one vital, practical question: *how* do we go about imaging Christ in our culture? To answer this question we must first understand the difference between the structure of culture in its various expressions and the spiritual direction that determines which kingdom it serves.

Structure and Direction

Imagine dozens of entwined electrical wires, encased together in a cord.[18] These wires are like the many aspects of life we experience. Together they constitute one whole structure. And that structure was ordained by God in creation. He structured by his word not just atoms and trees and galaxies, but societal and cultural life. All creation, existing as a response to God's laws, expresses his creation order.

Thus the various strands of our lives function alongside each other within the structure God has ordered. And they are many: physical, emotional, biological, intellectual, political, aesthetic, economic, ethical and devotional. Now these aspects by no means exhaust all that contributes to the structure of life—God's creation is too complex for that—but life seems to involve *at least* these dimensions.

Unlike the wires within a cord, however, the strands of life are not discrete parts. We can't separate them one from another; we cannot make an economic choice, for example, without reference to ethics, politics or intellect. We live them all together.

As wires do not exist for their own sakes, so the elements of life exist for a purpose. They are fields of activity. Electricity runs through the wires. God didn't create the world to be neutral, like a still-life picture.

In the beginning the current ran through his structure in perfect response to his creational covenant. Life moved according to the will of God—and it was good, says Genesis. Mankind (and all creation) served God in loving obedience.

Then sin came. It was a current running in the opposite direction. Sin didn't change the structure of life in the world; God's original creation continues to stand as he upholds it. What changed was the *direction* of the current.

God's work in salvation is to redirect the current of our lives. Redemption is the restoration of our obedience to the will of God, essentially our re-creation; the current runs in the original direction again so that we can be what we were meant to be.

Although obedience and disobedience may be compared to currents running in opposite directions, the comparison goes only so far. For life is complex. Good and evil are both present in God's creation. And the two kingdoms, or currents, are at war.

But notice that sin is not intrinsic to creation. It is never a strand of life in itself. The current of power does not flow one way in some aspects of life and the opposite in others, for good and evil are not structural parts of creation. God created *all* things good. Evil is the kink in *every* wire, in *every* aspect of life; it is the direction of current away from God into disobedience.

To think of some parts of life as good, as innately Godward in direction, and to consider others as by nature inferior, is to divide the structure of life into impossible categories. Such thinking is the basis of a sacred/secular dualism which reads good and evil into separate aspects of God's creation. Isolating some of the strands, it elevates them to a place of privilege—while depreciating others.

This is not the biblical view. Scripture suggests rather a certain "democracy" about the wires. Whatever sacred/secular or holy/common distinction may have been in force under the old covenant (with its special priesthood, Temple and sacrifices), all has been changed with the coming of Christ's kingdom. We need to heed Zechariah's prophecy of the Messianic age:

On that day "HOLY TO [YAHWEH]" will be inscribed on the bells of the horses, and the cooking pots in [Yahweh's] house will be like the sacred bowls in front of the altar. Every pot in Jerusalem and Judah will be holy to [Yahweh] Almighty. (Zech 14:20-21)

All aspects of God's world are created good, but all aspects are also fallen. In Christ all may be redeemed.

What does this mean for our practical, day-by-day living? It means that we as Christians must seek to understand cultural phenomena and to bring them under the lordship of Christ. Of each part of life we must ask two questions. First, what in it is creationally good? Second, what in it is *not* good? In what ways has it been *mis*directed?

These questions apply to every area of human culture. We may not simply write off an aspect of human culture as if it were beyond redemption, nor may we accept it uncritically at face value. Instead we need to struggle discerningly with our brothers and sisters in Christ (as well as with unbelievers who are sensitive to creational norms). We need to listen to God's Spirit as he points us back to the guidance of his word for all areas of our life.

PART 3

The Modern World View

CHAPTER 6

The Problem
of Dualism

The biblical world view of creation, fall and redemption is comprehensive. It tells with clarity and richness who we are, where we are, what is wrong and what the remedy is. It is a vision that illuminates literally all of life and empowers us to walk obediently before the Lord. Indeed, Christ's lordship will settle for nothing less.

But there is a problem somewhere. If a world view is always incarnated in a way of life (and it is), why do we find such a gap between our way of life and the biblical world view? The vision of life in the Scriptures has never been fully manifested in our cultural history. Somewhere its power has been short-circuited.

Is the "Christian" World View Biblical?
We could state the problem this way: Jesus said the kingdom of God is at hand, and that message is the heart of our gospel. But, as Jim Wallis

notes, "there is little evidence in the way Christians live to support our claim that the Kingdom of heaven is at hand. Rather, the evidence would suggest that, in most churches, the culture of economic, political and military systems of the United States is at hand. The question must be asked why the churches do not live by their confession."[1]

Where then *is* the gospel? Where is the good news culturally incarnate? If the kingdom of heaven is at hand, why don't the poor hear some good news for a change (Lk 4:18-19)? Why aren't captives set free? Why do the blind of this world still not have eyes to see? When will the downtrodden be given back their dignity? How do we account for our failure, as members of the body of Christ, to exhibit the attributes of citizens of the kingdom? Why doesn't the word *Christian* conjure up images of people turning the world upside-down?[2]

The problem is evident in every area of our lives. It has led some sensitive Christians to a crisis of confidence, some even to deny and abandon their faith altogether. If the biblical world view is unique, and if it is radically different from the dominant world view in our secularized culture, then why do Christians fit so well into our culture?[3] Why doesn't our life of discipleship and obedience make us appear as cultural oddities?

Perhaps this problem also accounts for the ineffectiveness of our evangelism. Are we embarrassed about our faith because we suspect it is irrelevant to unbelievers? After all, our lives differ little from theirs.

Notice how the apostle Peter responds to these problems: "Always be prepared to give an answer to everyone who asks you to give the reason for the hope that you have" (1 Pet 3:15). Peter assumes that people are asking questions of Christians. "Why do you people live the way you do? Why do you share your possessions with one another? Why don't you bow the knee to Caesar?" As they ask these questions, we are to be ready to give an account of our hope. In this context evangelism will be fruitful.

Perhaps people are not asking these kinds of questions because they don't notice anything significantly different about us.[4] Our lifestyle doesn't make them jealous of the gospel (see Rom 11:14). Unfortunately, when non-Christians do take notice of us, they are often repulsed by certain aspects of our lifestyle.

If we recall the criteria by which world views are judged (chapter two), it becomes evident that our problem represents nothing less than a world view crisis. A world view must elucidate or open up all of life. But the "Christian" world view operative in the churches often appears to be irrelevant to most of life. It is only concerned with our "spiritual" lives. Does our world view sensitize us to justice and oppression, as the biblical world view demands? The absence of most evangelical Christians from inner-city neighborhoods, peace marches and political actions striving for love, justice and mercy suggests that our world view is inadequate.

More important, however, is the question of whether the world view is consistent with its faith commitment, whether it is culturally incarnated in a way of life both whole and healing. At this point our world view crisis becomes acute. Not only does our world view seem irrelevant to most of life, but its very irrelevance suggests that it is a betrayal of both the Scriptures and our confession of Jesus Christ's lordship over all of life.

Split Vision

Where did things go wrong? How did our world view, evidenced in our way of life, come to be at odds with the Scriptures? The answer could be summed up in one word: dualism. Dualism is a split-vision world view. It separates reality into two fundamentally distinct categories: holy and profane, sacred and secular.

Now there is a world of difference between *dualism* and *duality*. Christian discipleship forces us to recognize duality in life: *either* we serve the Lord *or* we follow idols. Dualism blurs the valid duality between obedience and disobedience because dualism identifies obedience, redemption and the kingdom of God with only *one* area of life. It sees the rest of life as either unrelated to redemption (or the sacred), or worse—under the power of disobedience, sin and the kingdom of darkness.

In the place of a biblical understanding of the kingdom of God as God's rule over all of creation, the kingdom is identified with what has been called our spiritual life. Most people consider the spiritual life to be something relating to prayer, Bible study, fellowship and evangelism. And in what cultural institution do these activities occur? In the church.

So the kingdom of God (or the sacred) comes to be identified primarily with the church, while the rest of life is seen as secular. When people begin to feel the limitations of such a sacred/secular dualism, they say that the gospel must be "made relevant" to the rest of society. But what they often mean is that one institution, the church, must be made relevant to the other cultural institutions (the family, school, state and so on). The dualism remains. We still have two separate institutions which must somehow be related. Life is still fragmented.

This world view is dualistic because it has superimposed on the structure of creation the "directional" question of obedience or disobedience. The dualist understands the good-evil distinction (which is really a question of obedience or disobedience) as a distinction within the structure of creation.

Picture again the electrical cord. Like the cord, life is one complex structure made up of many strands, spheres of activity. On each wire the current can be positive or negative. Just so, the current of our activity may be either obedient toward God's creational laws or disobedient. Dualism, however, confuses structure and direction. Rather than seeing how the directional question runs through *all of life,* it identifies the direction with *particular parts* of the structure. Some aspects of culture are viewed as irredeemable (that is, inherently disobedient), while others are open to redemption. Such dualism distorts our lives because it distorts reality.

Dualism is not only a theoretical problem for professional theologians. It is *the* fundamental world view problem which has plagued the history of the church and still plagues us. A person with a dualistic world view simply assumes that life has two distinct realms. As James Olthuis says in *Out of Concern for the Church,* "This is his way-of-looking-at-things. No matter what he does, he does it within and from out of this 'two-realm' view. This view becomes his 'guide' in creation."[5] Dualism shows up in at least three ways: how we view work, how we view culture and how we read the Bible.

Christians and Work

Perhaps you've had the experience of going to a missionary conference and coming away with terrible guilt feelings for working at a "secular" job and *not* going to the mission field. Somehow we feel like second-rate Christians. John Stott suggests that we have created a hierarchy in the Christian community:

> We often give the impression that if a young Christian man is really keen for Christ he will undoubtedly become a foreign missionary, that if he is not quite as keen as that he will stay at home and become a pastor, that if he lacks the dedication to be a pastor, he will no doubt serve as a doctor or teacher, while those who end up in social work or the media or (worst of all) in politics are not far removed from serious backsliding.[6]

We have developed a notion of "full-time Christian workers." We are all embarrassed by the phrase (that's why we always put quotation marks around it), but the belief persists that only some of us are "full-time Christian workers."

This notion will continue to persist so long as our world view is dualistic. If the world really is split into two realms, one more important than the other, one more spiritual and more pleasing to God than the other, then we will always have a vocational hierarchy in the Christian community. Even when we reject this notion of full-time service and say that all Christians are full-time servants of the Lord, an unconscious dualism may still constrain us. We often mean that we are all called to evangelize, no matter what situation we find ourselves in. In this case submission to Christ may still be limited to a so-called spiritual activity that is unrelated to the actual work of a secular occupation.

The problem isn't that the Christian community is lacking in doctors, farmers, business people or musicians. The problem is that there are so few *Christian* doctors, farmers, business people and musicians. Most of us are Christians *and* something else; we do not engage in our daily tasks integrally as Christians.[7] Or we attempt to live an integrated life without abandoning our dualism. In this case we become doctors or farmers on the mission field, but we fail to develop a Christian alternative in medicine and agriculture.

Or we become a Christian business person—someone who runs a religious bookstore or makes lots of money in a secular firm and then gives that money to assorted Christian ministries. The question of how one "Christianly" sets up a business seldom goes beyond the basic moral questions of honesty. Seldom does the Christian ask foundational economic questions: What is the purpose of business enterprise? What is the role of profits? Will my particular enterprise be both ecologically sensitive and socially responsible?

Similarly, a Christian musician may feel limited to singing religious or "spiritual" songs, remaining out of touch with music that deals with the whole of life. This notion of Christian music usually leaves no place for instrumental music, apart from accompanying a singer with a "message." Such noble but misguided attempts at integration stem from a split vision of life. These well-meaning Christians are merely adding faith to their vocation rather than letting their faith transform their vocation. A dualistic framework will never provide impetus for such transformation.

We experience our work life dualistically even apart from this question of how it relates to our faith. Indeed, most people in our culture have a clear dividing line between their work life and their leisure life. Work is something we have to do, a necessary evil. It is worth doing, however, because it gives us the necessary resources to engage in the other activities we enjoy more. That part of our life is called leisure. In contrast to work, we are "free" during our leisure time—free to play, free of any constraints from our employers.

The Ancients and Work

The roots of the work/leisure dichotomy go all the way back to the Greeks and Romans. Cicero said that the "toil of a hired worker, who is paid only for his toil and not for artistic skill is unworthy of a free man and sordid in character."[8] The issue wasn't the toil per se but whether the toil was freely chosen.

Commenting on the Greco-Roman view of work, political scientist Paul Marshall says, "What was objected to was work and relations based on dependency and necessity—the absence of autonomy."[9] Consequently, different kinds of work were rated according to the level of freedom and necessity involved. The more freedom and the less necessity, the better. Aristotle, for example, ranked shepherds high because their work has a higher level of leisure (free time) than other kinds of farming.[10]

This freedom/necessity dualism in the ancient world implied that most of the work in the empire was done by slaves and servants. Free people, by definition, were not supposed to engage in the sordidness of necessary work.

Augustine (354-430), the giant of the church fathers, also maintained a clear dualism on the subject of vocations. He did not say secular occupations were totally out of bounds for Christians, but he did suggest that farming, the military, law, sailing and trade were but "rivers of Babylon." They would pass away. They were temporal, not eternal. Consequently, one could not truly exercise a Christian calling in any of these occupations.

The Greek freedom/necessity dualism became for Augustine the distinction between the "contemplative life" *(vita contemplativa)* and the "active life" *(vita activa)*. The latter included all manner of "necessary" work, and the former was the domain of reflection, meditation and prayer. Marshall remarks, "While both of these kinds of life were good, the contemplative life was of a higher order. At times it might be necessary for one to have the active life, but, wherever possible, one should choose the other; 'the one life is loved, the other endured.' "[11]

We can see how this contemplation/action dichotomy corresponds directly with the leisure/work dualism. Much later Thomas Aquinas (ca 1225-74) confirmed the *vita contemplativa/vita activa* distinction, identifying the former with an orientation to the eternal and the latter with the necessities of the present life. Although both have their place, he argued, contemplation is a higher calling than the life of action.[12] Consequently, the monastic or priestly vocation was the only true Christian calling. "In fact the term *calling* or *vocation* was only used to refer to such pursuits," says Marshall.[13]

So the distinction between "full-time Christian work" and "secular occupation" is merely the modern Christian version of the work/leisure, necessity/freedom dichotomy. Originating in Greek thought and adapted by the church fathers, dualism has remained with us. Even though it has no scriptural support, it permeates our consciousness—and therefore our world view.

Christians and Culture

A dualistic world view makes a Christian cultural witness problematic at best, impossible at worst. Earlier in this chapter we asked why Christians in our society tend to fit in so well. The answer is dualism. A dualistic world view splits life into sacred and secular realms, and most human culture gets identified as the realm of the secular.

Those who hold such a world view inevitably have trouble relating the sacred to the secular; they cannot maintain an integrally Christian cultural presence. Most Christians today identify the sacred solely with their personal and individual life, so that their faith has less and less to do with the culture "out there." Christians have little influence in shaping culture because their world view precludes such an influence. If, by chance, Christians do find themselves in positions of cultural leadership, often their Christian faith plays only a minor role in guiding their decisions.

Let's keep in mind, however, what we mean by *culture*. We do not mean that sphere of high matters relating only to leaders, artists, politicians and writers. No: we are *all* cultural creatures. The question of culture, as we have seen, concerns how we bathe our babies, educate our children, spend our money, entertain ourselves, form our marriages, do our work, structure our worship, cast our votes and approach our studies. Culture forming is our God-ordained creaturely task. Unfortunately, Christians have been culture followers rather than culture formers. How can we reverse this?

Here, in biblical language, the question is, how do we live *in* the world without being *of* the world (Jn 17:16-17)? The Israelites had to deal with the idolatrous nations around them; the early church faced the Greco-Roman culture; and now we face a deeply secularized society. This is the "world" problem; it is fundamental to our "world" view. Indeed, we could say that the way a Christian defines the "world" is a sure tip about the kind of world view he or she maintains.

Within a dualistic framework, Christians see the world in one of three ways: either as second best in comparison to the life of faith, or as an unavoidable evil, or as something to be fled. H. Richard Neibuhr in *Christ and Culture* identifies these three positions respectively as "Christ above culture," "Christ and culture in paradox" and "Christ against culture."[14] To get a sense of the differences among these three positions, let's imagine how each would deal with whether children should read "secular" novels in school. The controversy over J. D. Salinger's *Catcher in the Rye* could be a test case.[15]

Those who hold the "Christ above culture" perspective would not likely be opposed to their children's reading such a book. As a cultural product and the result of human imagination, novels (including this one) are good to read. Children should be taught that cultural pursuits are good but that the pursuit of holiness is a better and higher goal.

The perspective of "Christ and culture in paradox" is similar, but there is a significant difference. Culture isn't good; it is a necessary evil. We should read novels not so much to enjoy them as to understand the world in which we live. This position forces Christians into a paradox: they lead *both* the life of faith *and* the life of the world. They have a negative evaluation of culture per se, yet they reject any escapist attitudes.

The more extreme position pits "Christ against culture." *Catcher in the Rye* is evil and children should not read it. If a school requires children to read it, then parents should withdraw them from the educational system.

These three perspectives have, in general, predominated in the history of the church.[16] But all three perspectives fail to offer a uniquely *Christian* cultural witness. Culture is always seen as something apart from the gospel and redemption. A positive Christian cultural presence or witness is never possible because the gospel is relegated a priori to only one area of life, while the rest of life is identified as the "world." The result is that either Christians live in their own well-fortified ghetto, or they serve the Lord in one area of life and follow other gods in other areas of life. In the latter case they attempt to live with a compromise which the Lord said was impossible; they try to serve two masters (Mt 6:24).

Because dualism identifies the world with an unredeemed part of life (distinct from the sacred, redeemed, part of life), the comprehensive scope of the biblical world view is denied. Macaulay and Barrs point out in *Being Human* that "the 'world' in the New Testament is the sphere of life in which God's lordship is rejected, where the things of this life become ends in themselves or even are worshiped."[17] Consequently, anything can be worldly, just as anything, in principle, can be redeemed by Christ. The question, therefore, which dualism always avoids is whether our cultural life and our culture forming is obedient. Does it follow idols or the Lord? "There is no neutral ground," say the authors.[18]

Our dualistic approach to culture plagues us another way, the way we relate evangelism and social action. Many evangelicals see that the gospel makes social action a Christian imperative. But fear of losing the gospel by focusing exclusively on social concerns makes them try to hold the two in a balancing act. They speak of caring for *both* the body *and* the soul, *both* the physical life *and* the spiritual life.[19] But as soon as we speak of both/and in these terms, we are acknowledging a dualism: we are seeing two fundamentally distinct realities which we must somehow put together again. Perhaps this isn't the harsh dualism of the past, but it is still a dualism. And it cripples our social action because such involvement is always subservient to the "higher" calling of evangelism.

The consequences of this attitude are quite unfortunate. Christians sometimes say that our primary goal is to change the individual, not the system.[20] The dualism persists: somehow our spiritual life can be separated from our cultural life, and that means we can work in the accepted system. At worst, such a perspective allows us to live in idolatrous compromise.

Howard Snyder is concerned by the dichotomistic tendencies in much of our thinking about the relation of social action and evangelism. He says that we need a "more comprehensive and penetrating vision."[21] The vision he calls for is the kingdom vision of the biblical world view, a vision that affirms the goodness of our creaturely tasks when redeemed by Christ. We hold to the authority and inspiration of the Bible. Why then hasn't the comprehensive vision of the Scriptures been evident for us as we read them?

Glasses That Distort Scripture

Even our reading of the Bible is influenced by our world view. The Bible always seems to say what we expect it to say; for some reason our theology is always legitimated by the Bible.

The problem is that people with extremely different theologies, even cults, make the same claim to biblical fidelity. This problem can be described as the hermeneutical circle; the text and the perspective we bring to it always seem to legitimate each other. The Scriptures, however, are a double-edged sword that can cut through this circle (Heb 4:12-13). They are useful for correction and reproof; they can shatter our dualistic world view and instruct us in God's view of the world (2 Tim 3:16).

An eschatological passage is a good test case because an eschatology is always implicit (and often explicated) in a world view. So if our world view is unbiblical, it will inevitably distort our understanding of the biblical text. The text at hand is Matthew 24:36-41.

No one knows about that day or hour, not even the angels in heaven, nor the Son, but only the Father. As it was in the days of Noah, so it will be at the coming of the Son of Man. For in the days before the flood, people were eating and drinking, marrying and giving in marriage, up to the day Noah entered the ark; and they knew nothing about what would happen until the flood came and took them all away. That is how it will be at the coming of the Son of Man. Two men will be in the field; one will be taken and the other left. Two women will be grinding with a hand mill; one will be taken and the other left.

You might now be expecting a defense of a particular eschatological theory (amillennial, postmillennial or premillennial), but our question is more simple. The punch line of Jesus' teaching comes at the end. When the Son of man returns, two men will be in the field; one will be taken and one left. Two women will be working with a hand mill; one will be taken, one left. The question is, Who is taken and who is left?

Perhaps you are already humming Larry Norman's song, "I Wish We'd All Been Ready." Many books have been written and films produced based on this text. Who is taken and who is left? Most Christians would probably answer, "The Christian is taken and the non-Christian is left, of course." But look again at the text. Why should we believe the Christian is taken? Does the text justify such an interpretation?

Seeing Scripture Anew

Let's look closely at what Jesus is saying here. The Son of man will come in a day just like the days of Noah. People didn't believe Noah when he was building the ark. *They* just went along on *their* merry way, and *they* knew nothing until the flood came and *took them all away*. Who got taken away? The people who ignored Noah! So also when the Son of man comes, some will be *taken away*. Who? The same kind of people as in Noah's day—*the ones who ignore the gospel of salvation* and persist in disobedience.

In other words, a close look at the text reveals that it isn't Christians who are taken away, but non-Christians. Rather than addressing the issue of the rapture of the saints, Jesus is here speaking of judgment on unbelievers. The parallel passage in Luke 17:26-37 is even more explicit. The disciples ask where the people are taken and Jesus answers, "Where there is a dead body, there the vultures will gather" (Lk 17:37). The message of judgment on those who are taken is unmistakable.

If the text is actually saying the non-Christian is taken, why then have we so consistently misread Jesus' words here? Why do we so desperately want to believe that the return of Christ results in the taking of believers out of creation?

Rather than seeing that the biblical vision of the future is a restoration of creation and of our creaturely life before the Lord, we seem to have substituted a dualistic eschatology which removes us from creation and places us in heaven.[22] Our dualism leads us to a world-flight mentality. It has closed our eyes to the biblical vision of heaven coming to us.[23] So we consistently misread passages such as Matthew 24:37-41.

Our world view affects how we see everything, even how we read the Bible. A world view that lacks the comprehensiveness of the biblical world view will necessarily cause us to misinterpret the Scriptures. It will always miss the full scope of their redemptive message.

Romans 12:2 speaks directly to our situation. "Do not conform any longer to the pattern of this world, but be transformed by the renewing of your mind." This verse suggests that we can be (indeed *should* be) transformed, and that it will occur as we renew our minds. How do we do that? Through letting the Scripture shape our world view. But we just saw that our world view in turn shapes our interpretation of Scripture. How do we break out of this hermeneutical circle?

Usually we don't. It sometimes takes a world view crisis. We must at least be open to renewal and growth. We must allow the Spirit to correct or even overthrow an unbiblical world view. The Scriptures are sharper than a two-edged sword and can shatter our preconceptions. The Holy Spirit, working through God's Word, can lead us in new vision and new obedience.

CHAPTER 7

The Development of Dualism

If it is true that Christendom has been plagued with dualism, then the first step to a restoration of the biblical world view will have to involve a better diagnosis of the origins of the disease. In chapter six we outlined briefly where this mode of viewing life came from, but now we must look at it more carefully. We will want to see, further, how this dualistic world view came to be the secular vision of life which guides modern Western culture.

The New Testament contains the earliest Christian writings we have. In it we read about the primary concern of the first generation of Christians—their conflict with traditional Judaism. Because Christianity began as a Jewish movement, this conflict was bound to arise. Issues such as circumcision, Jewish ceremonial law and the relation of Gentiles to the church, therefore, occupy many pages of the New Testament.

Conflict with Judaism, however, was not so important for the second, third and fourth generations. The culture within which the gospel had to take form was both Judaic and Hellenistic, but it was the Hellenistic environment that demanded the most attention. And it was Hellenism that was to have a crippling effect on the life of the church.

Plato: Soul versus Body

The two most important figures in the Greek philosophical tradition are Plato (ca 428-348 B.C.) and Aristotle (384-22 B.C.). Although Aristotle carried a lot of weight in the late medieval church, Plato was more influential in the first and second centuries of the Christian era. And by A.D. 100 (five hundred years after Plato), Platonic thought was experiencing a revival.[1]

The fundamental difference between Plato and Aristotle is captured by Raphael in his sixteenth-century painting *The School of Athens.* Commenting on the painting in *Escape from Reason,* Francis Schaeffer notes that "Aristotle is spreading his hands downwards while Plato is pointing upwards."[2] Aristotle emphasized the study of reality as we empirically experience it. Plato, however, "despaired of finding anything real in a world of instability and impermanence, and concluded that reality was not made of changing things. Reality was composed of unchanging ideas or ideals that Plato called 'forms.'"[3] These conclusions of Plato were to exercise profound influence on the development of early Christian thought.[4]

Foundational to all Platonic thought is its dualism, the distinction just noted between unchanging ideals ("forms") and the world of the unstable and changing ("matter").[5] Heaven is the true and ultimate reality, and earth is a derived reality—sometimes seen as an illusion, but always viewed as of lesser value. At its worst, Platonism viewed the visible world as "the homeland of evil," while it saw the world of ideas as the goal of human life and morality.[6] Following Platonic logic, we must deny our creaturely life in the world and strive for the heavenly life of permanence, stability and bliss.[7]

In his book *Phaedo,* Plato talks about the relation of body to soul. Two worlds exist within the human person, he says. "The soul is most like the divine, and the immortal, and the intelligible, and the uniform,

THE DEVELOPMENT OF DUALISM

and the indissoluble, and the unchangeable; while the body is most like the human, and the mortal, and the unintelligible, and the multiform, and the dissoluble, and the changeable."[8] The body is the "prison house" of the soul; it defiles the soul and inhibits the soul's ability to know the divine. Therefore the soul yearns to be released from its captivity in the body.[9]

This extreme dualism was the intellectual climate within which the faith of the early church had to be proclaimed and formulated. How would the church relate to this Hellenistic world view? Responses varied. They ranged from outright rejection (Tertullian, ca 160/70-215/20) to conscious accommodation (Justin Martyr, ca 100-165). The predominant pattern, however, was cautious acceptance.

By the third and fourth centuries the attitude that governed the thought of Christian leaders such as Clement (ca 155-220), Origen of Alexandria (ca 185-254) and Basil of Caesarea (ca 329-79) was that Greek philosophy was preparatory for Christian theology. Reading Greek philosophy was considered of great worth to the Christian, not as an end in itself but as a training ground for the higher task of biblical exegesis.

The early church fathers certainly rejected elements of the Greek philosophical tradition when necessary to affirm biblical truths such as the Incarnation and the spontaneous creation of the world.[10] Nevertheless, they tended to accommodate themselves to the Greek world view, and they began to read the Scriptures using dualistic world view glasses. We saw the consequences of that accommodation in chapter six.

A common allegory was used to justify this accommodation: like the Jews fleeing from Egypt, Christianity must carry away the gold and silver vessels of the enemy and employ them for its own use.[11] Greek philosophy was the gold and silver. The problem, of course, was to determine which were jewels worthy of use and which in fact were time bombs set to destroy the Christian world view from within.

One of the problems early Christians found with Plato was that he was too rationalistic. The heavenly ideals or forms were grasped by rational or logical thought. This left no room for revelation. The Neo-Platonism of the Greek philosopher Plotinus (A.D. 205-70), solved this problem. In Plotinus, both a certain mystical tendency in Plato and his dualism came to their highest expression. Plotinus, many Christians felt, left room for revelation precisely in his emphasis on the mystical transcendence of our creatureliness (including our reason) to a union with the Supreme Being. The dualism of the spiritual versus the material was now set in the Western intellectual tradition. [12]

Augustine: Eternal versus Temporal

Dualism received its ultimate theological legitimation with Augustine (354-430), who was heavily influenced by Plotinus. [13] The famous Plotinus scholar A. H. Armstrong comments: "The Western Neo-Platonic tradition deeply influenced St. Augustine, who read the *Enneads* in a Latin translation by Marius Victorinus, and principally through him the thought of Plotinus exercised a great and fruitful influence on Western Catholic theology and philosophy." [14] The question is whether this "fruitful influence" bears good or bad fruit.

We have already seen (chapter six) how Augustine's view of work and vocation had inherited Greek dualism. His view of soul and body was similarly Neo-Platonic. Although he doesn't depreciate the body to the extent of Plotinus (who at some points was even more negative than Plato), Augustine nevertheless fails to see the human person as a whole. Rather, he speaks of the rational soul "inhabiting" the body. [15] Consequently, it is the matters of the soul that deserve our highest attention.

Augustine's dualism leads him naturally to a rather negative view of sexuality. Indeed, most Christian dualists have difficulty affirming the goodness of human sexuality. Augustine maintains that Adam and Eve could have had sexual intercourse in paradise without sin, but he finds it hard to imagine the goodness of such sexual activity after the Fall. All sexual acts, even within marriage, says Augustine, are shameful because they are inevitably rooted in lust. That is why such acts are done privately and in the dark. [16] Augustine's view of sexuality was certainly influential. Although his writings were not the sole basis for the medieval rule of celibacy for the clergy, his views were often used nonetheless to exhort celibates to remain in that state. If sexuality is denegrated, then why should those with a religious "vocation" desire it?

As a Platonist, Augustine believed in a split between the realm of the eternal (or spiritual) and the realm of the temporal (or material). The soul finds its home in the eternal, and the body in the temporal. Knowledge is primarily a matter of the soul. Therefore, sensory perception may be real, but it neither gives knowledge nor has any ultimate worth. That is why Augustine said, "I desire to know God and the soul. —Nothing more?—Nothing whatever."[17] Indeed, for Augustine, any knowledge that was not of direct relevance to this "theological" knowledge was of no interest. Not only did faith have priority over reason, but reason's only valid task was to prepare us for faith and then to help us understand our faith.

In many ways Augustine is the father of the Middle Ages. The Augustinian world view permeates all of medieval culture. It is above all else "ecclesiasticized": the church dominates the whole society. That the institutional church should have inflated importance is inevitable when the realm of grace is limited to one's spiritual life and the church is seen as its custodian.

If the gospel is not seen as a reforming and redeeming power in *all* of life, then the church as custodian of that power will extend its influence, often at the expense of the rest of life. It will take sole charge of education, for instance, whether in monasteries or in cathedral schools. And church-state conflicts will occur, as the church will constantly be asserting its superiority over the secular state.

This last conflict points to the implicit hierarchy in all dualism. The dualist sees all social order in terms of higher and lower institutions and classes.[18] Because of the Platonic distrust of change and development (heaven, after all, is stable, immutable and unchanging), this social hierarchy is also static. In God's providence people are placed in their "station in life," and any attempt to move into another vocation is strictly forbidden.

Indeed, such a static culture will disallow any economic or technological innovations which might upset the status quo of the social order.[19] A culture with a "vertical" orientation to heaven will, in fact, have little impetus for economic, technological or scientific development. A Platonic concern with the forms or ideals will preclude any real interest in the material world. The vertical orientation of life necessarily devalues the horizontal orientation.

Aquinas: Nature and Grace

While this Augustinian Platonism set the pattern for medieval thought and culture, in the late Middle Ages another philosophical movement arose which attempted to place more emphasis on the natural and horizontal side of life, albeit still within a dualistic framework. Western Christianity had come, through the crusades, into renewed contact with the philosophy of Aristotle. In fact, during the twelfth and thirteenth centuries his texts, acquired primarily through Islamic contact, were translated in a flurry of activity. The appeal of Aristotle, after centuries of Platonism, was his empiricism. His writings on logic, physics, medicine and biology excited people who had been limited to the realm of the eternal for so long. Aristotle replaced Plato as "the philosopher" in many Christian writings.

In this revival of Aristotelianism we meet Thomas Aquinas in the thirteenth century. While Augustine stressed the fallenness of humanity and nature, Aquinas stressed their created goodness. Although he thought human reason was still inferior to divine revelation, he nevertheless affirmed reason as a true, if insufficient, guide to attaining truth about our natural experience. With this affirmation of reason Aquinas also affirmed the validity of natural and social life. "All these [natural] activities were indeed subordinated by him to the supernatural vocation of man, and were raised to a higher power by the Christian's supernatural end of action, but they had their own reality and value, they were not mere shadows or vanities."[20]

Aquinas affirmed nature, but he did so within a dualistic framework. Once dualism had come into the church via Plato and Plotinus, it would take more than a new empirical emphasis to exorcise it. Aquinas's view of the relation of the gospel to life was that grace functioned as a *donum superadditum* (a "gift-added-on-top-of") to nature. According to Aquinas, mankind was created as a rational soul in union with a body but he was *also* endowed with a supernatural gift of grace. This gift, given at creation, enabled him to know and love God.

The Fall into sin meant primarily the loss (or deprivation) of this gift. Humans are no longer in a right relation to God. But it is only the supernatural gift that has been lost. Human rationality in relation to natural reality and natural law is left intact, although weakened. Redemption in Jesus Christ, therefore, is the regaining of the *donum super-additum*. The original higher gift is restored by grace, via the church. Consequently, Aquinas could embrace Aristotle as a true and reliable guide in the realm of nature and could affirm the church and the Word of God as a supernatural addition and complement of our creaturely lives. He was Aristotelian (in the natural realm) and Christian (in the realm of grace).

For Thomas Aquinas, nature is the "independent 'stepping-stone to grace,' the substructure of a Christian superstructure."[21] The problem with Aquinas is that he retains an internal split in the creation "by distinguishing the natural and the supernatural and by restricting the scope of fall and redemption to the supernatural."[22] In terms of the biblical world view, he fails to grasp the radicality of Fall and redemption. Sin, like leaven, permeates all of creation. Redemption, however, restores all things. According to the biblical world view, grace doesn't "complement" nature; it "restores" nature.

The dualisms of Aquinas and Augustine are different, but they are both dualisms nonetheless. Aristotelian or Platonic, both are Greek in origin, not biblical. This history of dualism up to the late Middle Ages is our legacy. And the problems of dualism are our problems. They create a plague that still afflicts us. Dualism distorts our reading of the Scriptures and hampers our lives of obedience. But the most devastating effect of dualism is that it necessitates a double allegiance. It forces us to serve two masters. With the rise of the secular world view, in reaction to the medieval Christian-Greek compromise, our problem becomes even more critical.

From Dualism to Secularism

What happened in the medieval synthesis of Greek and biblical thought was a confusion of what we have called structure and direction. God's good creation structure was overlaid with the two ultimate directions possible within that creation: obedience and disobedience. Instead of affirming that good and evil are possible in every area of our response to God, the nature/grace dualism essentially placed the first direction (goodness, obedience, God's kingdom) in the realm of grace and placed the second direction (evil, disobedience, the world) in the realm of nature. Good and evil were thus structurally *fixed* into two separate realms. The realm of grace corresponded to the life of faith, personal morality and ecclesiastical affairs, such as worship and the sacraments. Nature enclosed all else.

Grace was thereby positioned *over* nature. The spiritual realm of ecclesiastical affairs was regarded as superior to the natural world and was thus more highly valued. This elevation of one dimension of creaturely life at the neglect and expense of the other was, in effect, a form of idolatry. As a result we find, for example, the extreme ascetic dualism in Thomas à Kempis's *Imitation of Christ,* which divinized the inward life and counseled escape from creation.[23] Or we witness the more relaxed, hierarchical dualism of Aquinas, with its emphasis on the neutrality or diminished goodness of nature and the religious superiority of grace. In these and other manifestations of the medieval world view we see the ecclesiastical aspect of life removed from its true context in the whole of life and idolatrously absolutized. Paradoxically, this led to disastrous consequences for the church.

The prime consequence was that it made the gospel irrelevant to life as a whole. In such a dualistic vision of life, Christianity has nothing essential to say to our "natural" life. If the gospel either repudiates creation (as in the ascetic version of dualism) or simply adds something extra to the "natural man" (as in the moderate Thomistic view), then the Christian faith affects creation and created life only *tangentially*. The radical, life-transforming power of the gospel is short-circuited.

Worse still, the way is opened for a double allegiance. If the gospel speaks no normative word for culture, then we will listen to some other word, for we are inescapably cultural beings. By leaving most of life unaffected by the claims of Christ, medieval dualism led Christians to find other ultimate authorities for the "nature" side of their lives. This became evident in the role that Aristotle and other classical writers came to play in late medieval and early humanistic thought. This kind of double vision leads to a form of dual worship. To this day Christians are still not free, in either their world view or lifestyle, from the debilitating effects of this unbiblical dualism.

The consequences of this dualism extend beyond the church, however. The church's dualism opened the door to the triumph of secularism as the guiding spirit of Western culture. To put it bluntly: if it were not for the medieval nature/grace dualism, *modern secularism might never have arisen at all.*

The French biologist-philosopher Jacques Monod echoes this historical judgment in his comment on the scientific revolution: "If this unprecedented event in the history of culture took place in the Christian West rather than in some other civilization, it was perhaps thanks, in part, to the fundamental distinction drawn by the church between the domains of the sacred and the profane."[24] While scholastic theologians had granted a limited degree of autonomy to the realm of our natural life, the Renaissance humanists so greatly expanded the autonomy of nature that there was no longer any need for the realm of grace. If God and Christianity were already basically irrelevant to most of life, why not make their irrelevance complete? In the words of Francis Schaeffer, nature had begun to "eat up" grace.[25]

This is not to say that the Western world view suddenly turned atheistic. Even to this day the proportion of strict atheists is not very high. Secularism does not necessarily mean lack of belief in God. It is more closely bound, as Bernard Zylstra points out, to the denial of God's revelation.[26] While God's existence is not necessarily questioned in the secular world view, God has nothing essential to say to us about what the world is like or about how we should live.

Secularism thus questions the authority and the relevance of God for the *saeculum.* This Latin word from which "secularism" is derived means literally the "age," that is, the created world viewed especially as temporal or historical. And it was precisely the realm of history, the temporal realm of everyday affairs, from which God was more and more excluded. As the *saeculum* was increasingly absolutized, God began to figure less and less prominently as an integral part of the modern world view. And man's position proportionally increased. We turn now to look at this new view of humanity, which is the heart of the modern world view.

CHAPTER 8

The Rise of the Secular World View

When did the secular world view first appear? To answer this question we would first have to ask a further question: when did modern European history begin? Unfortunately an exact answer is not possible; dating historical periods courts subjectivity and oversimplification. But it is fair to say that between 1470 (the origin of the Italian Renaissance) and 1700 (the beginning of the Age of Enlightenment) the "modern" world was born. In the fifteenth century, Europe could still be characterized as genuinely medieval, but by the eighteenth century modernity had set in.

What had changed? If we were to compare the modern Western world with medieval Europe (or indeed with non-Western cultures), the distinguishing feature of the modern West would be its secularism. The process of modernity has been the process of the increasing secularization of life. But what does it mean when we say that the modern world is essentially secular? For most people it means that modern people have lost interest in religion. We have moved from being a two-dimensional (secular *plus* sacred) to a one-dimensional society. We have lost the sacred.

This, however, is definitely *not* what we mean by secularism. Such an interpretation makes sense only within a dualistic framework in which the sacred and secular are separated. But neither do we mean by secularism a philosophical or intellectual system of beliefs (as we find, for example, in *The Humanist Manifesto*); it is not "secular humanism." Rather, we use *secularism* to mean a world view—that pre-theoretical, committed vision which has shaped the dominant institutions of the modern Western world since the Renaissance. The world view of secular*ism* is inevitably incarnated in the progressive secular*ization* of culture.[1]

While intellectuals by no means created the secular world view, they have nevertheless often been eloquent voices for the developing vision. To some of these key people we now turn.

Homo Autonomous

The essence of the new world view is captured in Pico della Mirandola's famous *Oration on the Dignity of Man*. Pico, writing in 1487, still largely within the Christianized Neo-Platonic framework of the Middle Ages, sounded the trumpet call of the modern, secular vision of humanity. In Pico's retelling of the creation story, God makes man indeterminate, without any specific nature. Then God addresses his new creation:

We have given you, Oh Adam, no visage proper to yourself, nor any endowment properly your own, in order that whatever place, whatever form, whatever gifts you may, with premeditation, select, these same you may have and possess through your own judgment and decision.

Gone is the fixed medieval order of society! In its place is modern humanity with unlimited possibilities. We can have what we choose; we can be what we will to be. God further tells Adam:

The nature of all other creatures is defined and restricted within laws which We have laid down; you, by contrast, impeded by no such re-

strictions, may, by your own free will, to whose custody We have
assigned you, trace for yourself the lineaments of your own nature.
Mankind—unlike nature—is thus neither limited by nor answerable to
the law of God. Instead of being a dependent creature, responding to
God's Torah in all creaturely activities, mankind is defined in terms of
freedom from law. Here we reach the core of modern secularism: the
postulate of *human autonomy*. In the modern world view, man becomes
a law *(nomos)* unto himself *(autos)*.

We could say that Pico's God, in effect, exempts Adam from creation,
from finitude. God tells Adam that he has no specific, limited nature,
"in order that you may, as the free and proud shaper of your own being,
fashion yourself in the form you may prefer. It will be in your power
to descend to the lower, brutish forms of life; you will be able, through
your own decision, to rise again to the superior orders whose life is
divine."[2]

So humans can become gods if they desire, for they are not bound
by the same creatureliness as the rest of creation. In these excerpts from
the *Oration* we can see how Pico was utilizing the concepts of the Neo-
Platonic, mystical tradition and yet was essentially speaking in modern
terms. Pico was sounding the death knell of the medieval world view.
Standing on the threshold of modernity, he prophesied of a new humanity to come, a humanity with infinite possibilities who would stand in
the place of God, whose destiny was in its own hands—*homo autonomous*.[3]

With the onset of secularism we thus have the transcendent realm
of grace reduced in secular terms to the human realm of freedom. The
basic dichotomy became that between free, autonomous man—the
rational subject—and determined, law-bound nature—the object which
exists essentially for human manipulation and control. But by this time
the very meaning of the word *nature* had changed. No longer did it
have the medieval significance of the nonspiritual aspects of life, including ordinary human culture. Instead it began to take on the modern
connotation of the nonhuman world, the realm of externality, of objects,
of resources to be exploited. Nature became the world "out there,"
distinct from—and in some sense opposed to—mankind. "Proudly con-

scious of his autonomy and freedom," suggests Herman Dooyeweerd, "modern man saw 'nature' as an expansive arena for the explorations of his free personality, as a field of infinite possibilities in which the sovereignty of human personality must be revealed by a complete *mastery* of the phenomena of nature."[4]

The Scientific Revolution

The mastery over nature first took form in the realm of science. Science, in the classical sense of the search for a systematic and abstract understanding of the universal structures of the world, did not begin with modern times. The ancient Greeks had already developed such sciences as logic, mathematics and astronomy. Yet their view of science, based on the dualism of a rational, transcendent, stable order and a chaotic, inferior realm of flux, was much more contemplative than was modern science. In short, Greek science was not particularly concerned with the empirical world. Its focus was on the abstract, rational structure of reality, and the permanent, stable laws and forms divinely implanted in the universe, which we could "plug into" by means of the divine part in us—our reason. Insofar as the human mind and the structure of the cosmos were both rational, science (although largely theoretical and speculative) was possible and justified.

With the coming of the Middle Ages, and the increasing spiritualization of Greek dualism, the empirical scientific enterprise became more inhibited. There was certainly a medieval consciousness of what we would today call nature, but this led not to modern science but to the observation of nature for a "higher" purpose. Even when viewed in a positive manner, nature was not seen as important in itself but only as pointing to God and the realm of grace. It consisted of illustrative material for homilies, moralizing and edification, or for the construction of a natural theology—evidence of God based on the order and harmony of the world.

A rising empiricism. During the twelfth and thirteenth centuries, however, this allegorical attitude became somewhat transformed. For example, Albert the Great, the teacher of Thomas Aquinas, traveled extensively on foot throughout Europe, investigating and observing his surroundings. He began to view creation as more than symbolic or illustrative. He was interested in the "natural causes" of things. Despite the imperfections of nature, Albert realized that its study was important both for its own sake and for its practical applications. Although Aquinas did not carry through in this empirical, practical interest quite as thoroughly, he nevertheless strongly emphasized the beauty and goodness of the world and combated extreme otherworldliness and contempt for this life.[5]

But these emphases paled in comparison to the importance of the empirical world in the fifteenth and sixteenth centuries. This was the age of exploration and discovery; the "new world" of the Americas had opened up. Human horizons were expanding, and modern science was on the upsurge. Indeed, science was to take the leading cultural role in the early development of the West. The new vision of human conquest and exploration of nature for our own ends soon embodied the power of scientific discovery and invention, and greatly contributed to the scientific revolution of the seventeenth century.

To get a flavor of the role of modern science in the developing secular world view, listen closely to the words of the inventor of the scientific method, Francis Bacon. Writing in his *Novum Organum* early in the seventeenth century, Bacon explained that "man by the fall fell at the same time from his state of innocence and from his dominion over creation. Both of these losses however can even in this life be in some part repaired; the former by religion and faith, the latter by arts and sciences."[6]

Bacon was a Christian, and he believed in the Fall. Yet the unbiblical nature of medieval dualism is evident in his separation of the "spiritual" and "natural" aspects of the Fall and in his proposal of a twofold means of salvation. In other words, Bacon's dualism required that he give two answers to each of the world view questions "What's wrong?" and "What's the remedy?" While the restoration of our moral innocence was in the hands of God, the restoration of our dominion over nature was, in Bacon's opinion, in our own competent hands.

Here we have an illustration of how the nature/grace scheme prepared the way for modern secularism. Because God had been excluded from a relevant role in our cultural, and specifically scientific, life, some other mode of salvation had to redeem our dominion over creation. Thus Bacon proclaimed instead an essentially *humanistic,* and thus secular, way of salvation.

Bacon was concerned, it is true, with the *restoration* of our pre-Fall dominion over creation. To this degree he still retained explicitly biblical elements in his world view. Yet, as historian of philosophy John Passmore has pointed out, "The idea of 'restoration' can be quietly dropped so as to leave behind it an ambition the most secular-minded of scientists could happily share."[7] The avowed purpose and ambition of Bacon's utopian scientific society in *New Atlantis* was "the knowledge of causes, and secret motions of things; and the enlarging of the bounds of human empire, to the effecting of all things possible."[8] And this human empire, the "empire of man over things," Bacon claimed, "depends wholly on the arts and sciences."[9]

Yet precisely because Bacon still has Christian remnants in his world view, the idolatrously *redemptive* significance given to science becomes evident. "What sin had shattered," comments Passmore,

> science could in large part repair: man could become not only the titular but the actual lord of nature. This was by no means the orthodox Christian teaching; it amounted to saying that *man,* as distinct from God, could bring the world into the ideal state which Isaiah had prophesied.[10]

The millennium was at hand, a millennium dependent on human effort. What we have here is clearly a variety of humanism, but a particularly modern variety. This is *scientism:* the absolutization of science, the elevation of human scientific prowess to a place of salvific or redemptive significance. In science do we trust! This is the clear application of the postulate of human autonomy to the conquest of nature by the scientific enterprise.[11]

Mathematical rationalism. These attitudes were by no means unique to Bacon. René Descartes, for example, the father of modern philosophy, agreed with Bacon's essential ideas. Writing in 1637 in his *Discourse on Method,* Descartes took issue with the speculative philosophy of the medieval scholastics. He proposed instead "a practical one which, by teaching us to know the force and action of fire, air, the heavenly bodies, the skies and all the other bodies that surround us," would enable us to become "the masters and possessors of nature."[12] This mastery is taken, by Descartes, to be the self-evident human task, and Descartes' own philosophy provided a solid buttress for this view.

What was this philosophy? And how did it lend support to human mastery over nature? In answering this question we come to an important difference between Bacon and Descartes. Although both philosophers accepted and believed in the ideal of our mastery and conquest of nature, Bacon had an overriding, empirical, down-to-earth emphasis, while Descartes upheld an abstract, philosophical, rationalistic position. Indeed, the distinction between empiricism and rationalism, although often overplayed, illustrates their different viewpoints.

For Descartes, mathematics (particularly geometry with its axioms and deductions) was the paradigm of absolutely certain, infallible knowledge. Therefore, from his own basic axiom *cogito ergo sum* ("I think, therefore I am") he tried to construct an edifice of philosophical knowledge by using rigorous logical steps. Starting from the internal world of pure thought, he attempted to bridge the gap to the external realm of objects. His success in this endeavor has been widely debated ever since.

What is generally acknowledged as an important contribution, however, is Descartes' now-famous division of the world into *res cogitans* ("thinking thing," or mind) and *res extensa* ("extended thing," or matter). By this rigid dualism he emphasized, even more than did Bacon, the radical gulf between man and nature. While man was a free, conscious, rational agent, all nature was but a grand machine, the realm of dead matter, functioning by ironclad laws of cause and effect which man could understand and exploit to human benefit. This is one of the origins of classical physics, and the Newtonian billiard-ball universe. Moreover, this Cartesian reduction of nature (that is, everything *but* the human mind) to *res extensa*—a system of physico-spatial, law-determined relationships (even animals were mere machines for Descartes)—lent support to the impunity with which autonomous humanity could manipulate and exploit the natural world for its own ends.

Descartes viewed the physical realm not in terms of the rich diversity and variety in nature but in terms of the abstract quantitative relations or laws by which the world-machine functioned. Although such ideas do not seem so extraordinary to us today, Descartes' new "mechanical philosophy of matter, motion, and mathematics" was by no means obvious to the people of his age.[13] It was a radically new, highly abstract conception of the universe, and it was quite distinct, for example, from Bacon's "common sense" view.

Bacon agreed with Descartes on the ultimate goal of science, but he found the Cartesian "mechanical philosophy" repugnant. Any science that departed from the clearly observable, empirical realm was suspect. The mind, important as it is, must be corrected by the senses, the final court of appeal. The direct observation of nature (and not mathematical calculation) was, in Bacon's view, the only valid route to true science.

It was precisely for this reason that Bacon rejected the Copernican view of the heliocentric universe, which had been gaining in popularity. This view was, in Bacon's opinion, simply speculative theory, too distant from observable physical facts. It tried to account for the motions of the planets by taking recourse to what Bacon considered an unverifiable mathematical system. Such a theory could not be part of genuine science.

A Humanistic Utopia

The central idea in Bacon's philosophy was *experiment*. In fact, the word itself came to have almost magical connotations among the Baconians of the later seventeenth century. Inductive experimentation was regarded as the royal route to understanding nature's secrets and attaining genuine scientific knowledge. This was Bacon's "new method." He envisioned a whole army of artisans, mechanics and technicians (untutored in, and thus uncorrupted by, speculative philosophy) who would employ this method for the control of nature and the benefit of mankind. Bacon's resounding call for this "democracy" of experimental scientists (a sort of scientific "priesthood of believers") was one of his significant contributions to the great advancement of science in the seventeenth century.

According to historian Richard Foster Jones, the tremendous emphasis placed on experimentation in seventeenth-century England, along with the view that science is to be harnessed for utilitarian or even utopian ends, is directly attributable to Bacon's influence.[14] The Royal Society, which was officially founded by charter in 1662 to encourage the advancement of science, consciously traced its roots back to Bacon, taking him as its mentor. He is even venerated in much of the literature of the period. For example, Abraham Cowley's preface to Thomas Sprat's *History of the Royal Society* (1667) "attributes the reformation in science to Bacon, comparing him to Moses, who pointed out the promised land, though he could not enter it himself."[15]

The religious connotations of this analogy are entirely appropriate, for a definite religious zeal was developing for the new science. Among the members of the Royal Society, notes Jones, "experiment and observation as the proper method for the discovery of natural truths represented a *faith*, to doubt which was heresy." And every new success of the Society "raised them [its members] to the highest pitch of enthusiasm and filled them with confident visions of the future."[16] In the eyes of the Royal Society (and their influence was spreading rapidly), science dispensed the sure word of knowledge, an omniscience which would lead mankind into the promised land, the humanistic utopia which was just around the corner.

The Baconian experimental method was a necessary, although not sufficient, condition for the development of scientism. This new idolatry also required Descartes' mathematically based, mechanistic world conception. Bacon had rejected the Cartesian mechanical philosophy; it was initially regarded by the Royal Society as an optional hypothesis, a theory to be tested by experiment. Yet it was precisely the Cartesian approach that "was slowly establishing science on the firmest foundation it had ever possessed."[17] Descartes' mathematical, quantitative emphasis proved extremely fruitful for the formulation of scientific "laws," and thus for the prediction of phenomena. Indeed, his reductionistic conception of a scientifically manipulated world-machine may be regarded as "the charter of the Industrial Revolution."[18]

Experimental empiricism and mechanistic rationalism *in tandem* constituted the impetus for the scientific revolution.[19] Together they provided a firm basis for the newly developing faith in a secular paradise attainable by human scientific and technical mastery of the natural world. Although this perspective was by no means unchallenged, either today or in the seventeenth century, "the Baconian-Cartesian approach to nature dominated the West, at first merely as an aspiration, eventually as an achievement."[20]

Science, Modernity and the Christian World View

Are we overplaying the negative elements of the scientific revolution? Was the initial drive behind the origin of modernity really so anti-Christian? Was there not, on the contrary, a significant *Christian* motivation behind the rise of modern science?

Certain Christians today emphasize that modern science began and flourished when it did because it was solidly undergirded by the Christian belief in a rational God who had created a rational universe which we could understand by the exercise of reason.[21] But is this really the case? First, is this an essentially Christian understanding of God and the world? And second, whether or not it is Christian, was this in fact the motivating force behind the rise of modern science?

The answer to each of these questions is both yes and no. First, the "rational universe" view is only Christian in the sense that it is one (rather unhelpful) way of stating the biblical teaching that God created the world with a lawful structure or order which exhibits his wisdom. These laws are primarily meant to be obeyed, but they can also be scientifically studied. Moreover, the idea of a structured cosmos with constant regularities is by no means unique to the Judeo-Christian world view. It is found also in the world views of other ancient Near Eastern cultures in Egypt, Mesopotamia and Babylonia.

Furthermore, the idea that this cosmic structure is essentially rational is a characteristically *Greek,* not Christian, understanding of the world. As mentioned earlier, Greek philosophers believed that a divine rationality (a *logos,* or the ideas of a divine mind) was implanted in the very structure of things, and that humans by their reason (the "god" within) could conceptually grasp this structure.[22] Although this rationalism generated much philosophical contemplation, it did not lead to empirical science because it was fixed within the context of a dualistic perspective that did not consider the physical world important enough for detailed study and observation. This dualism, with its rationalistic overtones somewhat softened, passed into and decisively influenced the medieval Christian tradition. Here too it produced much philosophical and theological speculation, but *no empirical science.*

It seems, then, that we need another hypothesis to account for the origin of modern empirical science besides the idea of an ordered universe which can be rationally studied. What is missing? Consider the striking image suggested by historian R. Hooykaas: "For the building materials of Science (logic, mathematics, the beginning of a rational interpretation of the world) we have to look to the Greeks; but the vitamins indispensible for a healthy growth came from the biblical concept of creation."[23] What was missing in the Greek and medieval world views, and what was new in the sixteenth and seventeenth centuries, was a positive appreciation of this world and of the human task in it.

The trouble is that there were two versions of this growing affirmation of the *saeculum.* Due largely to the Reformation's emphasis on the Scriptures, the biblical vision of God's good creation and of the cultural mandate to develop that creation was recovered.[24] On the other hand, the Renaissance proposed a secularized version of this affirmation. God's good creation was reduced to a machine, an object that humans could manipulate; and the God-given task to develop creation as stewards was transformed into the humanistic vision of our autonomous scientific conquest of the world-machine. Because a new positive appreciation of the world is found in both the Reformation and the Renaissance, it is difficult to determine if Christianity is primarily responsible for the development of modern science.

The secular world view is, in fact, based on the reality of a good creation and the cultural mandate. Thus the answers the biblical and secular world views give to "Who are we?" are amazingly similar. But there is a profound difference as well. The Scriptures proclaim that we are God's special creatures, made in his image, created as stewards to develop his creation in humble obedience to his sovereign will. Secularism, on the other hand, repudiates any such submission to what it takes to be an external authority.

Yet the modern world view *does* quite clearly accept and forcefully emphasize the rightful authority of mankind to make use of and transform the created world. In this it is similar to the biblical world view and quite unlike the world views of many older, traditional cultures. Modern people do not consciously project their imaging function onto external idols set up as gods. In fact, they view their secularity and supposed nonreligiousness as one of their most significant achievements compared to previous ages.

Stewards or Gods?
In spite of its cultural triumphs and lack of classical idols, however, the modern West does not recognize man as God's image. This would admit both our inherently *derivative*, dependent nature and the *normed* character of the cultural enterprise. Consequently, the idea of stewardship is conspicuously absent from the modern world view. But if modern people neither see themselves as the image of God nor uphold external blocks of wood and stone as putative images, what options are left?

Here we come to what is absolutely unique about the modern secular world view. For the first time since the Renaissance we have in the West a whole civilization gradually coming to the belief and assertion that humankind itself is God—we need neither God nor images. The essence of modern humanism is that humanity deifies itself. This is considerably more radical than the Greek view in which man was divine by virtue of his reason, through which he participated in an eternal *logos*, or divine mind. Even the Greek view held a higher realm to which it was our duty to conform. In the secular world view, however, we find the amazing belief that man really *is* the measure of all things, and that the task of cultural development is therefore self-directed, normed by our own autonomous rationality.

From a Christian perspective this historical development is both strange and paradoxical. The paradox is the similarity, yet profound difference, between the world views of the Bible and of our modern time. But it is precisely because the secular view of human mastery over nature is so similar to the genuine biblical vision of the stewardship of creation that the modern age has enjoyed such incredible cultural advancement. The secular world view *is* dependent on an important biblical insight. Yet this insight has been terribly distorted.

To postulate our absolute authority over the *saeculum,* to suggest that we can by our own efforts, by virtue of our autonomous reason, control and manipulate external nature to produce a history, progressing from chaos toward an ultimate state of perfection and harmony— this is nothing short of a pseudoreligion! With humankind as god, and nature as the pre-existent stubborn matter we must subdue in order to bring forth our creation, there is even a secularized redemptive history and an eschatology of progress toward a final state of blessedness. The modern world view is a religion that has borrowed much from its Christian heritage but is itself nothing short of *idolatry:* man himself has become the idol.

In biblical terms, we have sown the seeds of our own destruction by breaking the creation covenant. As we saw in chapter four, idolatry always entails disobeying the laws of the rightful King, and the inevitable result is the judgment curse. Western man is now caught up in his idolatry. If we pursue our God-given rule of creation as if we are *owners* and not stewards, and if we engage in cultural development without obeying God's wise and loving standards, the result will be disaster —a world of war, hatred, lust, greed, competition, imperialism and environmental destruction. We are indeed finding, in these anxious days, that professing to be wise we have been fools. Disregarding the word of the Creator, we are being exposed in the depths of our folly. Such is the strange paradox of the Christian inspiration, yet humanistic perversion, of the modern age.

CHAPTER 9

The Gods of Our Age

The dominant Western world view has rejected the authority of God or gods and has affirmed the self-norming autonomy of humankind. Yet in spite of its humanistic and secular essence, Western culture *has,* in fact, served other gods, many of them—good, created things which we have idolatrously absolutized and religiously pursued in the hope of ultimate fulfillment.

Among these many idols, three in particular have emerged dramatically as central in recent history. This should not surprise us. Even though Western civilization is undeniably polytheistic, it could never have attained its cultural cohesion and dominance without some unifying absolute or absolutes. Without some prominent values to which we could be strongly and communally committed, without some major deities in which we could put our trust and around which we could orient our lives, it would simply not make sense to talk of *the* modern world view—or of Western civilization, for that matter. And while we may be experiencing today the disintegration of this very world view and civilization, there is still a dominant "orthodoxy" which has decisively shaped our history, and which lives on amid the crumbling ruins of our age.

In what follows it is not our aim to provide an exhaustive analysis of the development of our secular religion. For our purposes a brief outline will suffice. Just as our preceding discussion of the scientific revolution and the origin of the modern world view does not pretend to be a comprehensive history, so what follows is but an overview. Our intention is merely to highlight the unfolding religious commitments of modern humanity over the last four hundred years. We will look at those false gods which have had the most formative and decisive impact on the shape and direction of Western culture.

At the pinnacle of the secular pantheon stands an unholy trinity, one god in three persons, one idol in three absolutes. The three absolutes are scientism, technicism and economism.

Scientism: Legs of Iron
Like Nebuchadnezzar's statue in Daniel 2, this idol is "awesome in appearance" (Dan 2:31). Representing the kingdoms which would rule on earth, the several parts of Nebuchadnezzar's statue were made of different materials: "The head of the statue was made of pure gold, its chest and arms of silver, its belly and thighs of bronze, its legs of iron, its feet partly of iron and partly of baked clay" (vv. 32-33).

The idol of our age is also made of several parts. Its legs, its supporting base, are of iron—the strong, invincible iron of human scientific insight, the ability to grasp conceptually (and thus control) nature. *Scientism* is thus the first absolute in our modern religion. It is the first false god in which secular man has historically put his trust.

Foundational to the modern world view is the deeply religious belief that human reason, especially in the form of the scientific method, can provide exhaustive knowledge of the world of nature and of mankind. Science becomes the source of revelation. Instead of the priest of the medieval period, the scientist clad in authoritative white dispenses "knowledge unto salvation." The original sin is no longer disobedience to God; it is ignorance, irrationality or misinformation. Lack of knowledge is the root of all evil. We see then, with Os Guinness, that a fundamental pillar of modern humanism "is the belief in science as the guide to human progress and the provider of an alternative to both religion and morals."[1]

Unlike earlier Greek rationalism, which elevated contemplative and theoretical reason to a place of ultimate authority, modern rationalism is committed to a reason oriented to *praxis*. It was Francis Bacon, after all, who coined the phrase "knowledge is power." Jeremy Rifkin comments that, for Bacon, "the first and last word of human experience stated simply is: to be human, we must be in control. Action, not contemplation, is the goal. Any action that leads to greater control over nature is beneficial."[2] And from the beginning of the modern era until today, the conscious purpose of science has been the utilitarian manipulation of the world-machine for human ends. By continuously applying science, the modern creed confesses, we progress steadily toward an earthly utopia, a millennial age of our own making.

Technicism: The Bronze of Power

This leads us to the second false god in which the West has put its trust, the second tier of the idol of our age. Like Nebuchadnezzar's statue, the belly and thighs of this idol are of bronze—the efficient, productive bronze of *techné*, the formative, technological mastery of nature. This *technicism* rests on the achievements of scientism. It translates scientific discovery into human power.

Although technological innovations were evident throughout both ancient and medieval history, they usually failed to find their way into widespread use. Their application was blocked by the twin obstacles of a dualistic world view and a static social order. In the modern era, however, no such barriers to innovative progress remain. Indeed we identify nations as "modern" only if science and technology take a leading role in their ongoing development. As early as the seventeenth century people were creating a powerful science-based technology. Motivated by the ideology of conquest and the growing aspiration of a secular paradise, they worked to improve life on earth through scientific control of the environment.

By the end of the eighteenth century, as Bob Goudzwaard points out, this initial aspiration based on the *possibility* of progress had become an absolute faith in the *inevitability* of progress. The two overriding components of this faith were "its revolutionary *power to action*" and "its emphasis on *technological innovation* as a source of progress." So great was this emphasis that technology became, in Goudzwaard's words, "a saving guide, a mediator between man and God. It was the dawn of a new world."[3]

The new world was, and is, the world of the machine. We have technicized and mechanized modern life. Rifkin reminds us that

we regulate our lives by a machine—the watch. We communicate by a machine—the telephone. We learn by machines—the calculator, the computer, the television set. We travel by machines—the automobile, the jet. We even see by a machine—the electric light. The machine is our way of life and our world view rolled up in one.[4]

Earlier we noted the tremendous importance of the mechanistic world picture for the rise of science and technology. But why is the machine so important? First, a machine is something we can understand. We can take it apart and put it back together. We scientifically create it and quantatively analyze it in terms of energy input and production output. But, more important, the machine increases our ability to control nature. The machine makes us more powerful because it makes us more efficient. And we are mesmerized by exactness. In our technicized age, "precision, speed, and accuracy are the premier values."[5]

The astounding fascination and salvific significance of technology in the modern age are wonderfully captured by Henry Adams in *The Dynamo and the Virgin*. Describing his experience of the gigantic machinery at the Great Exposition of 1900, Adams writes that he experienced

the forty-foot dynamos as a model force, much as the early Christians felt the Cross. The planet itself seemed less impressive, in its old-fashioned deliberate, annual orderly revolution that this huge wheel, revolving at arms length at some vestigenious speed and

barely murmuring—before the end one began to pray to it.[6]
The motif that had guided Western culture for centuries had been exchanged for a new model. Faith that had bowed to the virgin with the
Child now paid homage to the machine. The sense of idolatry is over-
powering.

Threatened by recent criticism and skepticism concerning technology, Gould Inc., a Chicago-based corporation, has produced a series
of "apologetic" tracts to justify their faith. The first booklet of the
series, *Technology: Abandon, Endure or Advance?* declares its faith on
the very first page. A headline in bold type proclaims: "We believe in
the promise of technology." Undoubtedly, the writer admits, the rapid
advance of technology has caused some problems. How should we
solve these problems? "Abandon, endure, or move forward with new
ingenuity? All history shows that only the third choice is tenable." "The
solution to the problems introduced by a technological advance," says
another bold headline, "is, *and always has been,* another step forward."

Such assertions abound in this sermon on technicistic religion. But
the clincher is the final paragraph. In a highly emotional climax, a sort
of secular altar call, the writer asks, "Can we be sure that science and
technology will find the answers? Can we be sure that solutions to our
problems exist? No, but we can be sure that nothing but science and
technology can find them, if they exist." Then in a final religious resolve,
set apart in bold type at the bottom of the page, we read: "To put it as
bluntly as possible: Science and technology must answer our problems.
If they don't nothing else will."[7]

While scientism holds out the promise of omniscience, technicism
offers us omnipotence. Modern humanity has come to believe in the
unlimited (and thus unnormed) advance of science and technology,
regardless of the consequences—social, environmental or psychological. We have come to believe that if it *can* be known, it *must* be known;
and if it *can* be made, it *must* be made. Science and technology have
become autonomous guides, lifted out of their place in God's creation
and absolutized, elevated into idols. Science, which dispenses the sure
word of knowledge, is the inexhaustible fuel of our inevitable progress,
while technology is its efficient and powerful motor.

Where is this monstrous engine taking us? What is the ultimate goal of our progress? The answer to these questions was given in the industrial revolution (from the mideighteenth to the midnineteenth century), with its revolutionary transformation of modern society through rapid urbanization and the development of the factory economy. The ultimate goal of progress was economic growth and material prosperity.

Technicism: The Silver of Profit

The third section of Nebuchadnezzar's statue (the chest and arms of silver) represents the second half of technicism—the profit to which modern technology has been turned.[8]

The organization of an entire society around the profit motive is startlingly recent. The very *idea* of material gain, explains economist Robert Heilbroner, was blasphemous to the world view of the Middle Ages, but "the broader notion that a general struggle for gain might actually bind together a community would have been held as little short of madness." Yet this is precisely what happened.

Capitalist society is fundamentally "activated by the chase after money." Once the market system came into existence and the abstract ideas of commodified land, labor and capital were invented, Western society, which had previously been somewhat static and traditional, "found itself powered by an internal combustion machine. Transactions, transactions, transactions and gain, gain, gain provided a new and startlingly powerful motive force."[9]

Like the advent of modern science, capitalism required the affirmation of secular life in order to grow and flourish. Moreover, in the context of a growing scientific and mechanistic world view, it was almost inevitable that the ultimate goal of life would be something which could be mechanistically produced and mathematically quantified—namely, economic growth. Furthermore, the emphasis of secularism on human autonomous self-expression through the control and exploitation of nature released people from any constraints on their acquisitive appetite.

Western capitalism has its religious roots in discovering natural laws. Both Jean-Jacques Rousseau and Adam Smith believed that the first and most important law governing human existence is that of self-

THE GODS OF OUR AGE

preservation or self-interest. Smith argued that as long as people obeyed the law of self-interest and rationally attempted to advance their own economic interests, society would flourish and economic prosperity for all would abound. Somehow the self-interested activity of autonomous individuals, concerned for their own gain and not for the public interest, would be led by an "invisible hand" to promote an end which would be beneficial for the whole society. Economic life in the marketplace has its own laws, Smith argued, and if left unfettered by religious or governmental regulations it will automatically act in the best interest of society as a whole.

Accepting self-interest and the autonomy of economics had profound moral and religious implications. Western society "chose to base itself on a motive only rarely acknowledged as valid in the history of human societies, and certainly never before raised to the level of justification of action and behavior in everyday life, namely gain."[10] What medieval people viewed as the sin of avarice, selfishness and greed had now become the religious foundation of the economic system.

The invisible hand proved to be, of course, not only invisible but also impotent. Child labor, unhealthy working and living conditions, the rise of urban poverty and the pollution of the environment, together with runaway inflation and unemployment, all suggested that the economic prosperity of capitalists serving their own self-interest did not necessarily lead to the betterment of society. In this context we witness the rise of Marxism. While Marx accepted the ideal of scientific-technological progress as the inevitable route to desired economic prosperity, he insisted that the proletariat (the owners of labor as opposed to the owners of capital) would lead a revolution through which power would be transferred to them. This would lead in turn to the communist state, where equality would reign. We have seen the impotence of Marxist dreams.

A less extreme response to the failure of the invisible hand came from John Maynard Keynes. Keynes's interventionist economics abandoned Smith's laissez faire approach while maintaining (like Marx) the ultimate goal of economic prosperity. He argued during the Great Depression that the government should intervene in the economy to stimulate growth and full employment. He encouraged such intervention even if it resulted in governmental deficits. Many Western countries since the 1930s have followed this approach, although in the '80s there has been a conservative reaction to it in countries like Great Britain and the United States. But while the strategies may differ, the same motive of economic growth drives all these economic systems—whether laissez faire, interventionist or Marxist. Indeed, to question the validity and usefulness of economic growth for its own sake is tantamount to blasphemy in the modern world.

Economism: The Golden Head

The final tier of our triune idol is the golden head of the statue—the sparkling, enticing gold of mankind's ability to produce wealth and maximize profits. "Gold," Christopher Columbus is reputed to have said, "is a wonderful thing! Whoever possesses it is master of everything he desires. With gold one can even get souls into heaven."[11] The golden head of the modern idol has indeed elicited the ultimate commitment of modern man. "A rising standard of living," economist John Kenneth Galbraith has rightly observed, "has the aspect of a faith in our culture."[12] Ron Sider is more emphatic: "The ever more affluent standard of living is the god of twentieth-century North America and the adman is its prophet."[13]

We believe in the promise of the golden god, and it has driven us to servile devotion because its promise is greatest of all. While scientism offered omniscience and technicism provided omnipotence, the god of *economism* (the absolutization of mankind's good ability to make economic choices) extends to all who listen the breathtaking promise of full and glorious material prosperity—nothing short of secular salvation. "Consume and see that this god is good."

These three gods together—and their triune promises—have dominated the modern age. "In our western civilization," comments Goudzwaard, "we have ... given our trust to the powers of economic growth, science and technique to lead us in all our ways."[14]

The three gods of the unholy trinity do not have equal prominence today. Economism is the chief idol. Products are still sold to us because they have been "scientifically tested." For years Nestlé sales agents in the Third World convinced uneducated mothers to use infant formula rather than breast-feed by visiting them dressed in the authoritative white coats of medical science.

But scientism is no longer the dominant god of the West. For that matter, neither is technicism. When it comes to either scientific research or technological innovation, the bottom line today is, Does it pay? Is it profitable? The older gods are still there, undoubtedly, and they provide the foundation for our economistic idolatry; but they are largely subservient to the economistic head of the idol. Today, profit maximization and economic growth reign supreme. "Our economic system appears to be wholly secular," notes Walter Wink, "but it bears the marks of a priestly religion."[15] It is priestly because it mediates our worldly salvation, the good life of increasing material prosperity and well-being. This is the definitive modern version of the utopia to which we are progressing, the promised land of wealth and economic security.

The Close of an Era

We are living in the "last days" under the economy of the unholy trinity. The promised land is just around the corner, and we are in the final stage of secular "redemptive history." Just as God the Father sent the Son to effect our salvation, and the Holy Spirit now dwells with us to apply that salvation to our lives in the here and now, so it is in the redemptive history of secularism. The absolutization of science in the Renaissance fathered a tremendous technology which brings salvation, and the blessing and presence of these humanistic deities are today mediated to us through the economistic consumer society in which we live and move and have our being. The high god, scientism, in its omniscience conceived a divine plan and sent the son of technical mastery to subdue nature for our benefit. Divine reason took on flesh in the scientific-technological conquest of the natural world.

When the disciples of the new religion gathered at the industrial revolution, the spirit of capitalism was outpoured. And now in these last days we are filled with this spirit and empowered to do mighty acts of production and consumption, looking for and hastening the day when the invisible hand will cause the blessings of the economistic age to trickle down to all nations. And in that day everyone, great and small, will have prosperity. From the beginning of time never has such a day been; wealth will cover the earth, and weeping and toil will be no more.

In the words of Canadian songwriter Bruce Cockburn, our modern prophets have offered us

something for nothing, new lamps for old,

and the streets will be platinum, never mind gold.

But as Cockburn continues,

Well, hey, pass it on.

Misplaced your faith and the candy man's gone.[16]

How the vision is shattered! The age of unlimited economic expansion is coming to an abrupt close. We are coming up against the limits of creation itself. God's covenantal curses are raining on our heads for our idolatrous disobedience. The secular gods have not delivered. When a culture's gods fail, the time is ripe for serious world view reconsideration.

To Crush an Idol

For a world view to lead people's lives it must give them a sense of identity and place, offer a framework for culture forming and place life in a context of hope. If it fails in these tasks, its adherents may find themselves in the throes of a world view crisis.

But world views are not shaken easily. Their religious nature makes them resilient to all forms of opposition. For example, Christians are rightfully shamefaced when Muslims remind them of the crusades, but if their faith is sound that embarrassment does not cause them to renounce Christ. However, if conclusive proof could be put forth to establish that Christ did not rise from the dead, then Christians with integrity would have to acknowledge with the apostle Paul that their faith was worthless and in vain (1 Cor 15:13-17). Our God would have failed us, and our world view would be fundamentally discredited.

What would it take to undermine the dominant secular world view? What would make the three-tiered idol of scientism, technicism and economism topple? With its head of gold, one would perhaps think

that an economic depression would severely shake this unholy trinity.
But not even the depression of the '30s had that effect.

The Great Depression was seen as a mere setback which required
little more than some minor adjustments. True, the "invisible hand"
was not working as well as it ought, but that could be remedied by the
more visible hand of government intervention in the economic system.
In the United States the secular faith was firm. With a bit of New Deal
economics and a war to stimulate production, technology and scientific
research, the whole system was back on the track to progress, affluence
and social harmony. Two world wars, Hiroshima and the Great Depression may have made some of the intelligentsia question "progress,"
but the dominant cultural mood still favored an economistic world
view.

In 1930, in the midst of the Great Depression, John Maynard Keynes
wrote an article entitled "Economic Possibilities for our Grandchildren," in which he said: "Avarice and usury . . . must be our gods for
a little longer still. For only they can lead us out of the tunnel of economic necessity into daylight."[17] And what is that daylight? For Keynes
it was none other than a return "to some of the most sure and certain
principles of religion and traditional virtue."[18]

In other words, Keynes hoped for a noneconomistic society, but
felt that the route to such a society was through service to the idol of
economism. If we could just appease this god awhile longer, it would
surely release us from our idolatry.

But Keynes neglected to ask two questions. First, will this god ever
be appeased, or will it always require new sacrifices? Second, can we
really extricate ourselves from serving the idol, even when it is no longer
useful to us?

The biblical appraisal of idols calls for more caution than Keynes
admits (see chapter four). Idols are never appeased. They always require
more sacrifices. Once we place our trust in them we become their
servants. We surrender our dominion over the earth as God's image-
bearers, and we ourselves are dominated by our graven image. Our
lives are transformed into the image of the god we serve.

If there will be a new society, as Keynes hoped, it will not arrive because the idol has been appeased but because it has been overturned. And such an overthrow may be imminent. We are caught in a no-win situation. Our unholy covenant is doomed because neither side can keep the obligations of the covenant. Modern society cannot continue to withstand the sacrifices that the gods require, nor can the gods deliver on their promise of the "good life."

Autumnal Chill

The evidence suggests that we are in a culture in decline, a culture losing faith in its underlying world view. As Langdon Gilkey has said, "An *autumnal chill* is in the air; its similarity to the chill in other periods of cultural decline is undeniable."[19] Of course, it is impossible to say *with certainty* that we are in a culture in decline. But we could say, with Gilkey, that it "feels" as if we are reaching the end of a historical era.[20]

The "autumnal chill" seems to be creating intense personal anxiety in our culture. Social analyst Jeremy Rifkin says, "The scientific truths and technological tools that were supposed to bring us an artificial world of increased security and comfort are now spawning a level of intense anxiety that is precariously close to getting into mass social hysteria."[21] He connects this cultural *Angst* with the breakdown of world views:

> When a particular world view begins to break down, when it can no longer adequately answer the basic questions to the satisfaction of its adherents, faith is broken, uncertainty and confusion set in, and the individual and the masses are cast adrift—exposed, unprotected and above all frightened.[22]

When people are in the throes of such a world view crisis, they lose hope. Perhaps that explains why only fifteen per cent of new parents in the '80s believe that their children will have a better life than they did, compared with eighty-five per cent of young parents in the 1950s.[23]

The cultural anxiety is well founded. Our gods have failed us. They promised exhaustive scientific knowledge but have delivered a mere quantification of life, the loss of any meaningful commitment or personal involvement in scholarship, and the eclipse of all experiences, beliefs or values which are not "scientifically verifiable." Rather than make us omniscient, scientism has closed us off from all forms of non-scientific knowledge. As Martin Buber has pointed out in his book *I and Thou,* a scientific culture relates to things (the "It") and consequently loses the relation to people (the "Thou").[24]

We revered science because it promised to make our life better. "History, however, has rudely awakened us from this Enlightenment dream."[25] In the Middle Ages theology was the queen of the sciences. When people began to question and distrust the priest, it was evident that the medieval world view was on its last legs. Today, the growing distrust of doctors and scientists suggests that the modern world view is coming to an end.

Bacon saw scientific knowledge as a power to manipulate the world for human good. The god of technicism promised that such scientific control would provide us with more freedom and more commodities to consume. This god, however, has also delivered something quite different. Rather than provide omnipotence, it has rendered us powerless before the complete ecological breakdown caused by industrial pollution, depletion of the resources necessary for life, and the threat of nuclear destruction. People have good reason to be anxious when they cannot feel safe about the food they eat, the water they drink and the air they breathe—all because dangerous, technologically produced chemicals have proliferated. Indeed, it is precisely the success of the technological domination ideal that now threatens our very life.

We are not surprised when psychologists tell us that many of their clients experience self-alienation. People often work at mind-numbing jobs in which they are replaceable parts of a production machine. Because of increased automation they are threatened with losing their jobs. They live in efficiently built suburbs where every house looks the same and where many people spend their leisure hours relating to even more machines (TVs, motorboats, stereos, cars, video games and so on). A psychological problem like self-alienation is often part of the sacrifice technicism requires. But people are beginning to question whether the sacrifice is worthwhile, whether the payoff is big enough.

It is not. Economism has also been unable to deliver on its promises. The god has failed us on at least three counts: economic growth has not brought happiness; economic growth has proven hazardous to our lives; and economic growth itself is now reaching its limit. Let's look at each of these.

No Utopia

People develop cultures and behave in terms of their "horizon of happiness," and the modern horizon of happiness is utilitarian. If we maximize utilities (profits, commodities, leisure time and so on) and minimize disutilities (pain, effort, work), then happiness should result.[26] But the plan hasn't worked! Indeed, economist Robert Heilbroner says that the present cultural malaise "reflects the inability of a civilization directed to material involvement—higher incomes, better diets, miracles of medicine, triumphs of applied physics and chemistry—to satisfy the human spirit."[27] Material prosperity does *not* bring human fulfillment or happiness. The Bible has proclaimed this message for centuries. Our culture is just beginning to learn, painfully, its truth.

The second failure of economism is closely related to the first. Economic growth fails to make us happy precisely because it brings so much pain into our lives. Isn't it significant that in affluent and industrialized cultures medical problems like cancer and obesity abound? Is it not the "liberal" economistic cultures that make a commodity of sexuality? Are these not the same "efficient" cultures that treat the elderly and the disabled as lesser members because they are no longer "productive"?

This failure of economism shows up in the Third World, where a great deal of poverty is related directly or indirectly to our affluence. They have some right to point an accusing finger. The trickle-down theory may sound appealing, but affluence trickles down slowly, and the gap between rich and poor (whether internationally, domestically or even in our own churches) never changes appreciably.

Nor has economic growth produced the social harmony it promised. It is interesting to note that the one province in Canada which vigorously advertises for social workers is Alberta, the province where economic growth (due largely to oil discovery) has been the highest in the country.

Economism has not only failed us; it has cursed us. But the most crippling of all its failures is the third, which strikes at the jugular vein.

Most of us know, at least intellectually, that Western culture is encountering the finitude of creation. We have come to realize that economic growth does have definite ecological, social and psychological limits. But we are just beginning to see the ramifications of these limits for our world view. In simple terms, the age of economic growth appears to be coming to an end, and with it comes an end to rising economic expectations (individually, nationally, globally). Indeed, we may now be seeing the end (or at least the radical transformation) of capitalism itself.

Robert Heilbroner observes that "expansion has always been considered as inseparable from capitalism. . . . Conversely, a 'stationary' nonexpanding capitalism has always been considered either as a prelude to its collapse or as a betrayal of its historic purpose."[28] An economic contraction of the kind the Western world is currently experiencing is not, therefore, merely an economic issue; it is one that strikes at the heart of our economistic culture. No wonder we have such widespread cultural *Angst* today!

In terms of all of the economic issues confronting our society (simultaneous inflation and unemployment, production slowdowns, government deficits, labor-management struggles and so on), the most important issue has been the energy crisis. Indeed, we could say that the energy crisis is a kind of crystallization point in our culture. The energy issue exposes our cultural vulnerability and displays the fundamental inadequacies of the Western world view.[29] Our preoccupation with efficiency has led us to develop energy-intensive production systems and lifestyles. (Machines, after all, can give more output per unit of energy and capital input than is ever possible with human labor.)

Our kind of economics made sense when cheap energy was abundant. Since the 1970s we have been rudely awakened from our dream. In a finite creation, energy is scarce and must be used responsibly. The scarcity of energy has therefore struck at the heart of our culture. A common metaphor now has the ring of truth: our cultural spirit is indeed "running out of gas." The crisis is so severe that many American leaders suggested during the Iranian revolution that a war over the control of Iranian oil fields was a distinct possibility. When people are prepared to die for oil, we begin to see how foundational such energy supplies are to their lives.

The new reality we face is the reality of limits. As Rifkin has said, "our expansionary value system no longer fits the reality of a physical world where absolute limits to growth demand a revolutionary accommodation in our world view."[30] No longer is it possible to view the multitude of problems that face us (from energy scarcity, economic contraction and inflation to nuclear holocaust, pollution and deteriorating relations with the Third World) as mere breakdowns in a machine that requires interventionist tampering. Our crisis is a world view crisis.[31] Listen to Harvard social analyst Daniel Bell: "The real problem of *modernity* is the problem of belief. To use an unfashionable term, it is a spiritual crisis, since the new anchorages have proved illusory and the old ones have become submerged." On the next page of his book *The Cultural Contradictions of Capitalism,* Bell goes on to ask, "What holds one to reality, if one's secular system of meanings proves to be an illusion? I will risk an unfashionable answer—the return in Western society to some form of religion."[32]

A spiritual crisis requires a spiritual solution. The demise of a world view requires the adoption or development of a new one. Both Bell and Rifkin suggest the possibility of a new reformation.[33] The question that Christians must ask is, What should the components of a renewed cultural vision be? Does the biblical world view shed light on our cultural malaise? Could it be the healing force in our culture today? We have diagnosed the disease and have seen that the prognosis is grave indeed. Can Jesus Christ, through his body, bring healing?

PART 4

The Biblical World View in Action

CHAPTER 10

A Christian Cultural Response

The brokenness of our present cultural situation calls for a healing response. For Christians not to respond would be inconsistent with the biblical world view and would constitute disobedience to our Lord himself. In the chapters on the biblical world view we saw that creation is God's; he will never give up on it. Jesus Christ is the one who restores the covenant between God and his creatures. There is no autonomy in the creation; everything is covenantally bound to the Creator.

We must remember, however, that all covenants have stipulations. If they are obeyed, blessings flow; if they are disobeyed, curses follow. In terms of its covenantal relationship with God, the Western world is now experiencing the covenantal curses which disobedience calls forth. We are in a period of judgment, though not the final judgment. We are still "between the times"; there is still time to repent. Indeed, such a judgment calls forth repentance, for we have no other viable option. The creation itself will force us to change our ways because it will no longer sustain our present cultural patterns.[1]

Fleeing from the world is no option for a Christian. As we saw in chapters six and seven, such a dualistic attitude is unbiblical, discredits the gospel and cannot really function as a viable world view. We live *in* this culture—there is no escape. Jesus' call for us to proclaim his kingdom means that his healing must be offered to our dying culture.

Perhaps the greatest problem with a Christian cultural witness is that evangelicals are often at the forefront of those who try to preserve the status quo and the capitalistic way of life. Such Christians may be opposed to certain elements in modern culture (abortion, liberalized education and so on), but they still want to conserve many of its central features, such as economic growth, technological superiority, militarism and free enterprise. Such a position is clearly schizophrenic. It attempts to uphold both the gospel of Christ and the cultural forms which exist in service of idols. This is a dead-end historically and theologically; these cultural forms cannot be sustained. A radically different cultural vision is required—one that is rooted in the biblical world view.

A Comprehensive Vision

This Christian cultural vision must be comprehensive. It is of little help to develop a Christian response to abortion if we don't also address the arms race. Such a narrow approach results in a contradictory Christian view of "moral" society, one that is *against* abortion and *for* increased military expenditures. Death is death; these two issues must be related.[2] Similarly, a response to secular values in public education and the problems of pornography and capital punishment, without seriously developing a Christian educational philosophy, and addressing the commodification of sexual life and the issue of penal reform, is unhelpful and shallow.[3]

Our approach must be comprehensive because all of the issues are interrelated. Environmental problems are related to industrial growth; unemployment is structurally related to automation and energy-intensive production; production processes are in turn related both to energy scarcity (which itself leads to international tensions) and to psychological problems in workers. And the list continues. Food shortages cannot be separated from unequal distribution of the world's resources or from agribusiness, which is related to both pollution and the demise of the family farm. A utilitarian notion of efficiency is connected to the way we treat the elderly and disabled, and to the way we "process" people through our social institutions (banks, schools, hospitals). The interrelatedness of the issues before us is unmistakable.

We, however, do not offer here *the* Christian cultural response, but rather *a* Christian cultural response. The Christian cultural response is the response of the whole church, and we are offering here our contributions to that development.

We take seriously Bob Goudzwaard's warning about Christian "blueprints" for society. Societies are dynamic; blueprints are static. A Christian cultural witness is long-term; blueprints are short-term. Cultures are organic; blueprints are mechanical. No, we don't need blueprints. What we do need is direction, what Goudzwaard calls signposts of the kingdom. We need some vision to direct us along the cultural path and through the present darkness.[4]

Like Nehemiah we have known judgment and continue to know it. But history has not ended yet, so we must try again to rebuild our culture. Just as Nehemiah began to rebuild Jerusalem, *we* are called to make a new attempt to be culture builders in covenantal obedience to Yahweh.

What will such obedience require of us? It will require that we meet four conditions. We must abandon our idols, recognize the multidimensionality of life, respond in obedience to God's norms for his creatures, and begin to live in community with one another in a renewed way.

Renouncing Our Idols

The first condition is perhaps by now obvious, but it bears repeating. If our crisis is spiritual, then we should begin to question whether our faith has been misplaced. Any god that cannot deliver on its promises is not worthy of our service. Goudzwaard says we "must call into question the claim of economic, technical and scientific progress to be its own justification."[5] We must be free to evaluate and even reject "progress."

Renouncing our idols, however, is not easy. Their power may be waning, but they do not willingly loosen their grip on our lives. We may affirm intellectually that happiness is not quantifiable or utilitarian, but we still accumulate wealth and consume commodities in a way which belies our intellectual knowledge and shows where our heart is. But unless we outrightly reject these gods, cultural renewal is not possible.

To approach ecological concerns from a self-interested, economic stance, for example, is self-defeating. If we conserve energy and clean up the environment simply because this seems to be economically necessary, then our motives are still rooted in service to economism. Such service will not help us out of this crisis. In fact, just such service gave rise to the problem. Similarly naive is the confession of faith we quoted in chapter nine: "Science and technology must answer our problems. If they don't nothing else will."[6] The spirituality of scientism and technicism is at the root of the problem, and it can hardly be the path to salvation. No, what we need is a rejection of these false cultural ideals.

We must start the discussion from a different place altogether. Rather than asking how we can stimulate the economy, Christians should ask a more fundamental question. Why should we hang on to the worn-out ideal of economic growth at all? And if we question economic growth, then we will probably question nuclear power as well—not because it is evil per se but because it functions as a basis for continued economic expansion regardless of the environmental and medical risks involved.

If we reject technicism, we will have to call for a new form of technology (because technique per se is not evil) which places people, not products, first. Or if scientism is seen to be a false god, then we will have to re-evaluate how we provide medical care in our hospitals and how we engage in research in our universities. These examples are not comprehensive, of course, but they show us what steps we might take if we choose to reject the unholy trinity.

Recognizing Multidimensionality

The problem with idolatry is that it elevates certain aspects of life at the expense of others. Consequently, the second condition for cultural renewal is that these other dimensions of life regain their proper role.

God's creation is multidimensional. All the assorted creatures and sides of life function in coherent interdependence. The science of ecology understands biological interdependence within creation, but what is true on a biological level is true throughout creaturely (and therefore cultural) life. Francis Schaeffer in his book on ecology said, "Thus God treats his creatures with integrity; each thing in its own order, each thing the way he made it."[7] If we were to take a similar stance, there would be serious implications for our lives.

The modern world view is reductionistic; that is, it reduces all of life to its economic, technical or scientific dimension. What would recognizing life's true multidimensionality mean?

Consider, for example, clothes and cosmetics. A Toronto magazine once featured an article on beauty schools where teen-age girls learn to apply make-up, color-coordinate their clothes and "look beautiful." This pursuit is not wrong in and of itself. Life has an aesthetic dimension which requires our consideration not only at the art gallery but also in our personal appearance. The problem arises when a teacher describes the "beautification" of her students as a way to help them "sell themselves," both in the labor market and in the never-ceasing hunt for a man (or men!). Not only is such an approach to clothing and make-up sexist, but it also reduces life to economic terms. Young women are "products" that need attractive "packaging" so they will "sell" well. A Christian cultural vision does not exclude fashion or cosmetics, but it does exclude an economistic reduction of our aesthetic lives.

Or consider labor. Human labor is understood in reductionistic terms as the efficient exercise of power to produce the maximum economic good. Such a view submits labor to scientific analysis to determine the most efficient way to accomplish a task. The worker is then told how to do that task, deprived of any freedom or responsibility.[8] In short, labor is submitted to *scientific* analysis, which determines *technical* efficiency in terms of *economic* production.

But work is in fact a multidimensional reality. Human beings are emotional, psychic and social creatures, and their humanity is belittled when they are given no freedom or responsibility in their tasks. Our work is not a separate part of our life; it is integral to who we are. And if our work cannot be an expression of our full personhood, we suffer emotionally. We find ourselves in the work/leisure dichotomy outlined in chapter six.

Labor also has an ethical dimension intimately tied to a worker's beliefs. If we, as Christians, believe that economic idolatry is rebellious to the God of creation and a sin against oppressed people of the world, then we will have to come to grips with an obvious problem: most of us work in institutions and systems which are erected in honor of this idol. Our Christian cultural vision will have to deal with this contradiction between who we worship on Sunday and what we serve during the rest of the week. Perhaps Christian union members, for example, should be urging their unions to be concerned not only with higher wages, but also with better pollution controls, labor-management relations and social responsibility. Taking such a stance would be more consistent with Christian stewardship of the earth's resources, and love and community in human relations. But the Christian worker must not be naive about the cost of ecological responsibility; it might require *lower* wages.

To recognize the multidimensionality of life requires that we give all aspects of life their proper place. Decision making, whether by governments or persons, should not be exclusively concerned with economic growth. In chapter one we reviewed the Canadian debate over the exploration and transportation of oil and natural gas in the Arctic. The government uses what could be called a two-track approach to the issue. The first and most important track is economic: what is the economic efficiency of any given project? Will the project produce the optimum economic benefit, using the best scientific knowledge and technology presently available to us? If the project passes this test, the decision makers proceed to the second track. Here they look to "minimizing" the social and environmental costs of the project.

Such a two-track approach to government decision making (whether related to energy, education, social policy or health care) fails to honor the integrity of the noneconomic dimensions of life. A Christian cultural vision, by contrast, insists that the social, environmental and personal issues are *just as important* as economic and technological considerations. So a two-track approach is always unsatisfactory—not only because it so easily sacrifices personal concerns, communities and ecosystems, but because it fails to respond to such norms as love, justice and stewardship. This failure leads us to our third condition for a cultural reformation.

Responding to God's Norms

Cultures express the highest values of the dominant world view. For example, people who value natural processes more than scientific analysis and technological control tend to favor natural and home childbirth; those who view pregnancy and birth as a medical "problem" often require the technological facilities and scientific expertise of hospitals and obstetricians. Our cultural approach to the biological act of giving birth, therefore, is related to our world view; different world views dictate different values or norms. They view "normality" differently. North Americans tend to consider the hospitalization of women giving birth as normal. But many other people consider it somewhat abnormal.

The home-birth movement gaining ground in North America collides with the dominant norms of the Western world view. But what is happening in this critique of birthing is happening throughout our culture. The "norms" of modernity are under fire. Why? Because our culture lacks some of the norms most essential for cultural life to continue. If a society is facing economic collapse, it is imperative that its people sacrifice some of their economic aspirations. But when our political leaders urge economic restraint, there is often an uproar from the population. Evidently our leaders are appealing to a norm that no longer exists in the hearts of our people.

Daniel Bell says, "Western society lacks both the *civitas,* the spontaneous willingness to make sacrifices for some public good, and a political philosophy that justifies the normative rules of priorities and allocations in society."[9] Autonomous man accepts no laws *(nomos)* or norms that infringe on his self-affirming, acquisitive freedom. Apart from the (so-called) norm of self-interest, capitalist individualism can have no norms.[10]

The problem is now reaching an acute stage, for we are coming perilously close to the point where the earth itself will *impose* certain norms on us. It is creationally unlawful to put chemical wastes into an ecosystem when they cannot be assimilated. If we persist in breaking such a law, eventually the ecosystem will break down completely and we will lose the resources essential to life. As we saw in chapter three, creation is law-bound. We are free to break those laws. When we do, however, the effects are tragic.

An obedient response to God's good creational norms is thus fundamental to a Christian cultural witness. Here the gospel of Christ can heal our culture. Many people see the problems but cannot provide any norms because they lack a biblical foundation.[11] They may know that utilitarianism is bankrupt, but their world view offers no alternative. The cultural opportunity for the gospel is greatest when people have no place to turn.

The tragic irony of the present situation is that people are desperately holding on to their hedonistic freedom, doing as they please, but the end result could well be the imposition of limits by an authoritarian state. If people cannot exercise internal self-restraint, then the specter of external control looms large. Robert Heilbroner's analysis of this scenario causes him great pain:

> The drift toward the strong exercise of political power—a movement given its initial momentum by the need to exercise a much wider and deeper administration of both production and consumption— is likely to attain added support from the psychological insecurity that will be sharpened in a period of unrest and uncertainty.[12]

The problem with an authoritarian state, however, is that it is by definition anormative. In totalitarianism the state *is* the norm, and it is subject to no norms outside itself. Heilbroner has good reasons to be afraid of the development of such authoritarian states in the Western world.

We do not question that there will indeed be a need to impose limits.

A Christian perspective, however, calls for both internal and external restraint. Cultural restoration is impossible without a renewed response to God's law. Just as the creation is multidimensional, so too is God's law. Rather than being an imposition on human freedom, his laws provide the context for our free and dynamic response.[13]

Goudzwaard calls for the "simultaneous realization of norms."[14] Not only must technological, scientific and economic norms be obeyed, but so must the norms of love, justice, mercy and kindness. Only if we attempt to realize all of God's norms simultaneously will we be able to rebuild our culture in covenantal obedience to Yahweh. Rather than postulating the goal of high production and consumption in a self-made secular utopia, we will seek to live whole, normative lives.

A "simultaneous realization of all norms" seems impossible. Doesn't high economic growth necessarily come into conflict with social justice? Yes it does, but perhaps our understanding of the norm for economic life needs to be rethought. God's laws are coherent. When they are properly understood, the norms of economics and justice function harmoniously. They are not meant to be played off against each other.

Let's take a closer look at the norm for economic life. In classical Greek two words describe economic activity, *oikonomia* and *chrēmatistikē*. *Chrēmatistikē* is "the pursuit of self-enrichment, for ever greater monetary possessions, if need be at the expense of others."[15] This characterizes our culture. It necessarily conflicts with norms of justice, love, community and kindness. *Oikonomia* (the root of our word "economics"), however, "designated the behavior of the steward whose task it was to manage the estate entrusted to him in such a way that it would continue to bear fruit and thus provide a living for everyone who lived and worked on it."[16]

Here, economics is stewardship. This is clearly how the Bible understands economic activity. Its purpose is twofold: it must responsibly nurture what belongs to the Master (a restatement of the original cultural mandate), and it must do so for the service of those who live on the estate (the whole human race, in that the whole creation is our Master's estate). There is no room in this understanding of economic life for individualism, greed, self-interest, exploitation or the idolatry of profits.[17] The doctrine of stewardship insists that economic activity is subject to norms which go beyond market share and profits. Thus a sensitive appreciation of stewardship leads us to question the role of private property in our culture (the steward *manages* property but does not *own* it), the destructive exploitation and wanton depletion of the environment (such practices are not ultimately fruitful, and the Master expects fruitfulness), the justification for multinational corporations (whose very corporate structure is self-serving and therefore in opposition to stewardship) and the unequal distribution of wealth. As Rifkin says, "The new stewardship doctrine turns the modern world upside down."[18] If economic life is guided by stewardship, then there need be no conflict with other norms, including social justice.

But our view of social justice, too, needs to be rethought. In the two-track approach to policy followed by political leaders, social justice is not only a secondary norm. It also suffers from an economistic interpretation. *To do justice* is understood to mean "to provide monetary compensation for injustice." The government takes away the land of native peoples and feels that justice is done when a generous cash settlement has been agreed to. Indeed, it seems that the most important issue discussed in our present legal system is not "What is justice?" but "What is a just settlement?" Justice is distorted when it is understood primarily in these economic terms, especially if our understanding of economic life itself is distorted.

The Bible often uses the words *justice* and *righteousness* interchangeably. To be just, therefore, can never be reduced to mere economic compensation. Nor is justice a matter of following the correct legal procedures which have been established by a consensus within society. Both societal consensus and legal procedures are unjust if they violate God's demand for righteousness.

We should listen to Jeremiah:

For if you truly amend your ways and your deeds, if you truly practice justice between a man and his neighbor, if you do not oppress the alien, the orphan, or the widow, and do not shed innocent blood in this place, nor walk after other gods to your own ruin, then I will let you dwell in this place, in the land that I gave to your fathers forever and ever. (Jer 7:5-7 NASB)

Jeremiah names the alien, widow and orphan as his examples because they are the weakest people in the society of ancient Israel. They have no means of livelihood, no place, no inheritance. And Jeremiah tells the people that *their* place, *their* inheritance of the land, depends on how they care for those who have no place. To do justice, in this instance, is to be a steward who assures that the blessings of the creation are shared by all. This is the economic side of justice. To whatever degree our political and economic structures inhibit such economic justice, they are unrighteous.

But Jeremiah's appeal is more than just a call for economic justice. Justice has to do with rights. If it is our creational right (and the right of future generations) to expect clean air and water, then environmental pollution is unjust. That is why legal regulations concerning the environment are just. Similarly, parents have a right to significant input into and control over the education of their children. Therefore, a centralized educational bureaucracy, over which parents have no control, is also unjust. And a laborer has the right to share in meaningful work. Any work situation that takes away the worker's responsibility infringes on that right.

A simultaneous realization of God's norms for our multidimensional cultural life would require vast changes in our society. Perhaps some of you are skeptical. "It won't work," you say. "Your analysis of our culture in decline has me so depressed that I can't even *imagine* our abandoning our idols, living multidimensionally, and trying to realize God's norms as we rebuild our culture. It's hopeless!"

If that is your response, then you have already anticipated the fourth condition of cultural wholeness—namely, community.

Renewing Community

Cultural anxiety easily gives way to a sense of powerlessness. Convinced that the idolatrous forces of destruction are living an independent life of their own, we stand immobilized, watching our world fall apart. It seems we can do nothing.

"How can I, one junior executive, begin to apply this Christian cultural vision in the multinational corporation for which I work?"

A doctor says, "I know that patients are treated as objects because the medical establishment has made gods out of the scientific method and technological efficiency. But what can I, one lonely Christian general practitioner, do?"

The answer? Nothing! By yourself you can do nothing in the kingdom of God. Just as our renewal in the image of God is communal, so our task of implementing a Christian cultural vision is communal. John Francis Kavanaugh has said that a Christian,

> in the face of our culture's dwarfing and isolating the individual, must turn to a community of shared life-experience which fosters committed faith and enables the individual to criticize and challenge the programming of the culture. The most effective means by which both goals are achieved is in a communally shared Christian life.[19]

We need community not only because the problems are so big but because we are the body of Christ. We experience our individuality primarily in terms of our unique contribution to the body.

Let's look at how the church can lay the foundation for developing and implementing a Christian cultural vision. In some provinces in Canada, for example, it would be illegal for a doctor to attend a home birth. So how can the Christian community help a doctor in its midst? First, the community is the natural place for the doctor to be challenged to develop a Christian approach to medicine. Second, the church community can support the doctor in his or her Christian medical witness as it takes shape. This support could even include providing financial, legal and spiritual help in cases where the doctor, for Christian reasons, transgresses what the medical establishment has set as the legal bounds for medical practice.

And the junior executive? The community should help business executives and laborers realize that they cannot simply function in the corporation as if there were no problems for Christians in that setting. Not that Christians should necessarily abandon their position in firms. Perhaps there are meaningful ways to begin to transform the situation itself. If, however, a Christian decides to leave the corporation, perhaps he or she could develop a new business enterprise within the community, one which operates on the principle of stewardship.

The community is God's means of empowering people. Our communal obedience to God's norms in all areas of life is a light to the world. The Christian community, with its biblical view of justice, should work for justice in political life. The church should be a place where the elderly and disabled contribute meaningfully. As a multidimensional community, it should be a place where the arts are encouraged and aesthetic life flourishes. (In these difficult economic times, the church might even financially assist its writers, musicians and artists so they can do their task in the kingdom of God.)

In short, the Christian community should foster a responsible economic lifestyle which radically breaks with the narcissistic consumerism that surrounds it. Christians need to develop ways of nurturing and educating their children so they will not be coerced into serving the idols of our age. It may mean establishing alternative schools.

When married people feel pressure to give up on their marriages as conflicts arise, the Christian community should provide a supportive and healing environment, perhaps even offering professional assistance. Similarly, we still need to work through what it means for women and men to be one in Christ. What are appropriate sex roles? What should the "liberation" of men and women mean in our community? These questions strike many of us deeply, and they cannot (ought not) be answered individually. They are communal questions.

What makes the Christian community Christian is its worship. A radical community, it subverts the dominant culture because it worships, serves and prays to a different God. Its worship sets the pattern for its whole life. Rather than being conformed to the world, it is a community being transformed by the renewing of its communal mind —its world view. Consequently its worship is not relegated to just liturgical activities, but it gives its whole life to God as a sacrificial offering (this is the point of Romans 12:1-2). Herein is the essence of a Christian cultural witness in a society in decline.

CHAPTER 11

World View and Scholarship

The Western world view has run its course. We are now in a period of cultural decline. Chapter ten argued that, from the perspective of a Christian world view, true cultural renewal is possible only if we abandon our idols, recognize the multidimensionality of life, respond obediently to God's norms for our lives and engage communally in cultural renewal. A Christian cultural vision must be comprehensive both because the crisis is so wide-ranging and because the Christian world view (by definition) addresses all of life. We turn now to see how our vision affects scholarship and study.

University Studies in a Declining Culture

Some might argue that in the face of such human tragedies as starvation, political oppression and the threat of nuclear holocaust, it is unconscionable for Christians to engage in the frivolity of scholarship. Why engage in studies when the whole of culture is in such a crisis?

Why indeed? Because the university is at the very heart of our culture. It is, therefore, a strategic place for a healing Christian witness. Moreover, unless Christians do some serious academic reflection, their cultural witness will lack both depth and insight. Such a lack is evident in many attempts at Christian cultural witness today.

If suburban shopping malls are temples of economism, and if the nuclear arms build-up is a sacrifice to technicism, then the university functions as the theological seminary for the high priests of scientism. Indeed, when we enter the area of scholarship we are entering, says Christian philosopher Hendrik Hart, "the sphere of influence of one of Western civilization's most dogmatic and influential religions."[1] If our analysis of scientism as one of the pillars of the faith of Western culture is fair, then we cannot avoid understanding the university in religious terms. Ideas developed in the academy are fleshed out in society.

Economics. Consider two prominent examples, first economics and then psychology. When a modern nation is in a state of economic recession, it turns to economic experts for a solution. (This is somewhat analogous to so-called primitive peoples turning to a local witch doctor to find out why the gods have not brought good crops this year.) If the economic experts (trained in the Western university system) adopt a neoclassical model of economics, they will advocate letting the market function independently (whether in terms of Adam Smith's *Wealth of Nations* or Milton Friedman's *Capitalism and Freedom*). Their answer will have definite economic, societal and ecological implications.[2] This laissez-faire approach not only results in high unemployment and environmental damage (environmental regulations are seen as "interventions"), but it also goes hand in hand with a weakening of social services. After all, if the economy is left to function on its own, say neoclassical economists, the material benefits will "trickle down" to the poor. Moreover, according to this theory, government assistance to the poor is economically counterproductive because it takes away their incentive to work.

If, however, the economic experts who are consulted in a time of recession are interventionists, a somewhat different situation emerges.

Interventionism, founded by J. M. Keynes (see pp. 137-38) and followed more recently by "liberal" economist J. K. Galbraith, also views the market as a mechanism, but it argues that the machine needs governmental maintenance. In this scenario, government expenditures and the national debt get larger and larger, while the role of government in the life of a culture moves ever closer to a benevolent totalitarianism. Interventionism produces, in the end, a welfare state.

We have here two economic theories that are developed, debated and taught in the comfort of the university classrooms, professorial armchairs and faculty clubs of our society. But the implications of these theories touch absolutely everyone's lives when they become normative in a given culture. Surely the Christian witness to God's norms for economics belongs in this theory-creating region of society.

Psychology. Now consider the well-known (and much-debated) behavioristic model in psychology.[3] Behaviorism understands humans exclusively through the model of stimulus→behavioral response→reinforcement. B. F. Skinner says that "man is a machine in the sense that he is a complex system behaving in lawful ways."[4] If the stimulus and reinforcement are consistent, the human behavioral response will be the same. In its Skinnerian manifestation then, psychology becomes the "technology of behavior"—a technology which can be used to manipulate people to behave in socially acceptable ways. Such behavioral technicism is the logical result of Francis Bacon's Renaissance view of scientific knowledge as control and power.

North American culture is nowhere near Walden II, but we can already see the cultural implications of such a behavioristic model. Government-sanctioned mental health hospitals, for example, regularly use behavioristic techniques in the care of the mentally handicapped. Further, the educational theory taught to the majority of our children's teachers is informed primarily by behaviorism. Our children's behavior and education, therefore, are "technically" controlled to the extent that their teachers follow this one model of psychology.

Advertising agencies are keenly aware of the way the right stimulus (audio or visual) and reinforcement can produce the desired behavior in a consumer. Corporate managers learn behavioristic tools to help in their "management" of staff relations and morale. Certain "incentives" (stimuli) and "affirmations" (reinforcement) keep the staff "productive" (the desired behavior). So even with this cursory glance we can see how one particular scientific theory, when it comes to have prominence in the academy, begins to shape the life of the culture.

Examples illustrating the way scholarship influences culture abound. Earlier we made reference to the medical profession. A model which sees the human body merely as a complex of biochemical functionings will produce the kind of drug-centered health care which characterizes Western society. Overemphasizing methods of quantification and statistics in academic sociology determines in the end what kind of social policy our government will adopt; it contributes to impersonality and coldness in our helping professions. If technique is absolutized as an end in itself, subject to no other norms, then automation, computerization and nuclearization will be our unquestioned symbols of progress.

A Christian Academic Witness
Because the university is at the "nerve center" of Western culture, Christians will be fully effective agents of God's healing kingdom in our declining culture only if they also bear witness and contribute there. But this is not the only reason for a Christian academic witness. If the university is indeed the place where we receive advance training in how to serve the gods of our age, and if education does in fact transform and mold our vision of life so that we serve as guides in a culture led by idols, then a Christian academic witness is imperative both for our *evangelism* and for our *pastoral* responsibility.

The evangelistic issue should be self-evident. The gospel must directly confront the religious direction of our age if it is to be effective. But we can't address the evangelistic task if the pastoral need isn't met first. That is, "Christians who are students" need to be led in their discipleship to become "Christian students."[5] Let's explore what this means.

The dualism we criticized so sharply in chapters six and seven is alive and well in the lives of *most* students who are Christians on North American campuses. As soon as one's faith is relegated to a spiritual realm of life (which may include campus fellowships, Bible studies and even evangelism), then the rest of life (the writing of term papers, exams and lab reports) is in principle free to serve idols. For instance, the Christian will write a term paper substantially the same way as his or her non-Christian classmate. Indeed, both students tend to have a basically utilitarian approach to a university education. They both want the academic degree because it is a ticket to a particular profession; and they both want a profession which will allow them to "buy into" the lifestyle and world view of the dominant culture. But we know that this culture, with its lifestyle and world view, is bankrupt. Consequently, by naively accepting the dominant world view in the university (an institution both formative and reflective of the culture), the Christian student is being unfaithful to Jesus Christ. That is why the problem is pastoral.

At the most foundational level, therefore, Christians must develop an integrative perspective in their studies. Jesus is Lord of all. His lordship is integral to all the student thinks and does. In the biblical world view the human cultural task (which includes scholarship) is both creationally affirmed and redeemed in Jesus Christ. The Christian academic calling is then to "take captive every thought to make it obedient to Christ" (2 Cor 10:5).

The years that a student spends in college or university are extremely important and formative for developing a world view. They provide young Christians with an opportunity to reflect on the meaning of Jesus Christ for their disciplines. Developing as "Christian students" (that is, students who think "Christianly") at college will set the stage for becoming a "Christian culture-former" for the rest of life.

Scientism Rejected

How does one start to develop as a Christian student? How do we gain a Christian perspective in our studying? Just as the first condition for cultural renewal is that we renounce the false gods which have failed us, so also in scholarship the first step must be prophetic: we must abandon the false god of scientism.

C. Stephen Evans has described scientism as "the belief that all truth is scientific truth and that the sciences give us our best shot at knowing 'how things really are.' "[6] Science thereby ceases to be a "very human enterprise" and somehow "exists" autonomously, apart from humans.[7]

Scientism is founded on the belief that rational thought is autonomous. Reason is considered a law to itself and therefore subject to no other law. Because autonomous science is absolutized science (it is scien*tism*), scientific considerations always have priority. This militates against the simultaneous realization of norms.

Implicit in this autonomy is the rejection of any role of religious belief in scholarship (see chapter eight). Science is seen as religiously neutral. Indeed, if someone introduces or suggests religious commitment in a scholarly discussion, it is routinely ruled out of order. Such commitment is seen as irrational. Yet Hart has noted the contradiction implicit in this rejection of commitment. Scientism claims that to be scholarly is to be committed to rationality. But this commitment is paradoxically not recognized as commitment. Belief in reason is exempted from being a belief. Scientism is thus blinded to its own religious nature.[8]

The late Dutch philosopher Herman Dooyeweerd exposed the "dogma of the autonomy of theoretical thought" as a myth as early as the 1930s.[9] This dogma has more recently been attacked by other Christian scholars such as James W. Sire, Nicholas Wolterstorff and Arthur Holmes.[10] It has also come under critical fire within contemporary philosophy of science, especially in the works of Thomas Kuhn, N. R. Hanson, Michael Polanyi and Gerard Radnitzky.[11]

If scholarship really is an activity that functions autonomously, unrelated to ultimate religious beliefs, then obviously there is no way to speak of a Christian perspective in scholarship. Nor would there be any foundation to our attempts at overthrowing scientism as a false god. But the fact is that science is *not* autonomous. The very proliferation of conflicting schools of thought in various disciplines, which find it impossible to communicate with each other, suggests that there is something more fundamental going on in these debates than mere conflicting interpretations of the facts. While Ian Barbour observes that there are no uninterpreted facts, Hanson points out that all data are already "theory laden."[12] And Dooyeweerd argues that debates between conflicting schools of thought are seldom productive because they do not penetrate to each other's starting points. Such penetration is impossible precisely because those starting points "are masked by the dogma concerning the autonomy of theoretic thought."[13] In other words, as long as we pretend that science is purely objective and contains no religious starting point, true scientific dialog is impossible. The dogma of scientism must give way to a fuller understanding of the religious nature of all scholarship.

From World View to Scholarship

James Sire has rightly argued that, in order to think, "we need a starting place, a place to stand, ground zero."[14] Wolterstorff says that "in weighing a theory one always brings along the whole complex of one's beliefs." The most important beliefs Wolterstorff calls control beliefs.[15]

Thomas Kuhn has given fresh insight to the issue of control beliefs by his discussion of "paradigms." For Kuhn, each scientific community (or school of thought) does its scientific work by means of a shared paradigm. The paradigm functions as the scientists' conceptual framework—their shared generalizations, values and beliefs. It provides the criteria by which theories are judged, evidence is deemed admissible, the nature of demonstration is determined, and the elements of a true conclusion are constituted. A paradigm suggests what questions should be asked and therefore which research programs will likely be fruitful.

A humanistic psychologist, for instance, may find research into mythical archetypes (á la Jung) to be promising, while a behaviorist would see such research as fanciful, not nearly so solid as data which can be quantified. Similarly, a doctor influenced by the holistic health movement may openly consider the therapeutic potential of acupuncture, shiatsu massage and homeopathy; but the traditional (shall we say, orthodox?) doctor influenced by the chemical model considers such methods unscientific, and those who practice them "quacks." Kuhn would comment that their "standards or definitions of science are not the same." The depth of difference between their paradigms is so great that, Kuhn says, "in a sense that I am unable to explicate further, the proponents of competing paradigms practice their trades in different worlds." Moreover, "the transfer of allegiance from paradigm to paradigm is a conversion experience that cannot be forced." Indeed, such a conversion, says Kuhn, requires "faith."[16]

We see, then, that scholarship is not a religiously neutral activity of "rational" human beings. It is fundamentally religious—for everyone, not just Christians. Arthur Holmes says, "Intellectual honesty consists not in forcing an impossible neutrality, but in admitting that neutrality is not possible. It consists in confessing and scrutinizing one's point of view and the difference it makes, and in explaining how other points of view would have to disagree."[17] Indeed, the fact that many (if not most) scholars are actually unaware of their point of view is one of the main causes of academic superficiality. With this superficiality ("I just look at the facts") comes the inability to be self-critical ("This is just the way things are") because such scholars never explicitly consider their starting points.

The relationship between one's ultimate religious faith as formulated in a world view and the detailed theoretical work of scholarship could be described as follows. All theoretical analysis, whether in the natural sciences, humanities or social sciences, occurs within the context of a philosophical framework or paradigm.

Here is how it works. Philosophy, like all academic disciplines, is theoretical in nature; but in contrast to the specific disciplines, philosophy is concerned with the totality of reality, not just specific aspects. As such it functions like Kuhn's paradigms. It provides a view of the whole of reality within which analysis of the parts occurs—"parts" like each of the natural sciences, humanities and social sciences. So the philosophical framework circumscribes the boundaries of a discipline, selecting what it will "see." If the scholar is self-aware, he or she shapes the discipline explicitly; if unaware, implicitly. The paradigm describes the relation of each discipline to other disciplines in terms of its basic understanding of how reality is structured and interrelated.

Let us suppose that Dr. X takes functionalism as his basic sociological theory. From this theoretical viewpoint, he understands society mechanistically. He sees how different social institutions *function* to maintain society. Thus, for Dr. X, "the individual is largely if not *completely* constituted by the social roles he plays."[18] For Dr. X, marriage is primarily a social institution, not an ethical relationship. To him the institutional church is a means of maintaining the status quo; it would never be a transforming force in culture. These are the "facts" that Dr. X sees and that he would set forth as a scholar.

All scholarship is undergirded by a philosophical stance. Dooyeweerd says that every academic discipline "presupposes a theoretic view of reality, including an idea of the mutual relation and interconnection which exists among its various aspects. And this idea, in turn, is intrinsically dominated by a central religious motive."[19]

Dooyeweerd has brought us back where we started. Our philosophical paradigm shapes what we see and "know," but it in turn is shaped by our basically religious answers to the four world view questions (chapter two).

The Bible often speaks of knowledge and wisdom in terms of obedience, relationship and intimacy.[20] Indeed, "to know" is often used in a way which seems synonymous with "to live." Such knowledge is *qualitatively* different from theoretical knowledge. To theorize is to stand back from something in order to objectify and analyze it. But knowledge in this biblical sense is pretheoretical. It is the base from which we spin our theories. Without a pretheoretical knowledge of life in its wholeness, we cannot even begin to ask theoretical questions about anything which is abstracted from the whole.[21]

Now we have suggested that the specific academic disciplines are distinct from philosophy because the former are concerned with particular aspects of reality while the latter is more encyclopedic in scope. Yet they share in common their theoretical nature. World views, in contrast, are not theoretical in nature; they are pretheoretical answers to ultimate questions. World views are not to be confused with philosophical systems, although both are views of the totality of reality. Rather, world views are foundational to such systems. They reflect what biblical writings often call knowledge.

Just as all scholarship presupposes a philosophical paradigm, so all philosophical paradigms presuppose a religious world view of one kind or another. We could diagram the progression from religious world view to scholarship (see figure 2).

world view ⟶ philosophical paradigm ⟶ academic discipline

| (pretheoretical view of the totality of reality) | (theoretical view of the totality of reality) | (theoretical view of particular aspects of reality) |

Figure 2.   From world view to scholarship.

A world view, or vision for all of life, is worked out in scholarly life, in the first place, when the scholar formulates a theoretical philosophical framework. Holmes says that "to think 'Christianly' is to think 'world-viewishly.' "[22] Only in this way can one's Christian faith function "internally to" scholarship, as opposed to being dualistically added "on top of" scholarship.[23]

The relationship between world view, philosophy and scholarship implies two things. First, if all scholarship is religious, then the Christian is not unique. Since scholarship is ultimately rooted in religious commitment (even if that commitment is to reason itself), then the question isn't really one of "integrating" faith and scholarship. Faith and scholarship always *are* integrated. The only real question is, *Which faith?* Many Christians, unaware of the implicitly religious nature of scholarship, find themselves doing scholarship from a faith perspective which is antithetical to their Christian faith. To do scholarship Christianly, then, is to consciously allow our faith to direct our studies. This leads us to the second implication.

If scholarship is in fact structured in terms of the world view-philosophy-academic discipline model, as advocated here, then Christian renewal in university studies will require some Christian philosophical insight. Without such insight a Christian academic witness will be piecemeal and superficial. One doesn't become a "Christian student" simply by applying biblical texts or Christian theology to his or her discipline. Wolterstorff comments that the Bible "does not provide us with a body of indubitably known propositions by reference to which we can govern all our acceptance and nonacceptance of theories."[24] Rather, the route from the certainties of the biblical vision of life to the details of specific scientific analysis is mediated by a philosophical paradigm. Therefore we need to develop such a theoretical framework, one which is sensitive to and rooted in the biblical world view. The final chapter will suggest the contours essential for such a framework.

CHAPTER 12

Toward a Christian Philosophical Framework

Cultural renewal is impossible until we have abandoned our cultural idols. Only then can we begin meaningfully to rebuild our culture. In a similar way our critique of the idol of scientism was a ground-clearing exercise for developing a Christianly inspired alternative in scholarship. That alternative also follows the same conditions as those outlined for cultural renewal: recognizing the multidimensionality of life, obeying God's norms for society and working toward a renewed sense of community. We will deal with the parallel of the "norms" question in scholarship before addressing the theme of multidimensionality.

God's Order for Creation
The Christian attempt at philosophizing begins with the perspective that everything, including humans and their theories, is subject to and

exists only in response to God's creational law (or word). All of life responds to and is dependent on God's norms. Thus all creation is "subjective" in the sense that it is *subject to* God's law.[1]

This subjectivity has immediate implications for a Christian academic perspective. Creation has a "reference character." That is to say, creation refers to, points to and is revelatory of its Origin. Theology has traditionally called this the doctrine of general revelation. The doctrine gives Christians a special impetus to study the creation. Of course, one could never replace the revelation of the inscripturated Word with the creational revelation. But Christian scientists should not feel that their scholarship is somehow second best to biblical scholars'. That would simply reinforce a dualistic point of view, which itself inhibits the development of an integral Christian academic witness.

If God's word orders the creation, then the scientific enterprise is best seen as a fallible attempt to formulate how his word in fact orders specific kinds of creaturely life. It must be noticed, however, that science has access to God's creational word only indirectly—by observing creation. So to understand how God orders biotic life, we engage in detailed analysis of patterns of regularity in actual, living organisms. Or if we want to know about the word of God for political life, we must not only study the Scriptures to see what they say about matters of justice and government, but we must engage in a detailed systematic and historical analysis of real governments and political theories.

Pitfalls in Legitimate Science

But this leads to three problems: (1) what we study is fallen, (2) the observable order in creation is often confused with logic, and (3) we who observe are ourselves a part of creation. Let's look at each of these.

Obviously no government perfectly represents God's complete mandate for political life. Only an idolatrous nationalism would make such a claim for itself. Creation is fallen, and its response is distorted and misdirected. God's word may be constant and sure, but the creature often seems to get it wrong. Christian scholars must therefore be critically careful in their scholarship to discern the universal effect of the Fall in creation as they attempt to develop theoretical formulations of the law for creation.

The second problem, however, is even more complex and controversial. When we in the Western intellectual heritage think of something which is "ordered" or "orderly," we immediately think in terms of logic. An ordered universe must be a logical or rational universe. But such an identification of creational order with logical order is in fact a result of a false allegiance to the autonomy of reason. This identification is based on the valid insight that logical (or theoretical) analysis has the legitimate task of formulating how God orders the creation. The trouble is that God's order for creation is not reducible to logic. Logic itself is subject to God's law or order for logical activity, just as aesthetic life, politics or social interaction are subjective responses to God's law for those aspects of life. To elevate logic to the level of the norm for all creation is implicitly to assert its autonomy, to deny that *all things* (including logical thought) are subject to God's law. God's word, which is full of majesty and power and has created and continues to sustain the universe, cannot be limited to what humans consider rational or logical.

As controversial as the distinction between the creational order and logic is, an even larger problem needs to be addressed. An incessant problem in Western thought and culture has been the tension between freedom and determinism. When the self-styled autonomous man attempts to explain, scientifically and mechanistically, all of reality as a "flawless chain of cause and effect," he leaves no place for human freedom. Dooyeweerd, describing this process, said, "Human willing, thinking and acting required the same mechanical explanations as did the motions of the machine. For if man belongs to *nature,* then he cannot possibly be *free* and *autonomous.*"[2] Here we find the profound irony of all allegiances to false idols. Promising freedom, the idols always enslave their worshipers. Western secular people believed that they had found the route to true freedom and "enlightenment" through their will to action and autonomous rationality, with which they would control their environment. But that very rationality in the end has threatened human freedom, because it has effectively submitted humanity to its own mechanistic analysis of nature.

How could human freedom be guarded? The nineteenth century sought to preserve human freedom by splitting the academic disciplines into two categories. Scholars wanted to stop the encroachment of the determinism they saw in the natural sciences lest it become the norm for *all* the disciplines of the academy. Consequently they cut the "humanities" off from the "natural sciences," and this division came to characterize the curriculum of Western universities. While the natural sciences attempted to "explain" natural reality in terms of strictly lawful relations of cause and effect, the humanities attempted to "understand" human reality more in terms of free human choices in history.[3]

Tentative "Laws," Free Universe

Understandably, this debate raises a question for a Christian paradigm which would emphasize God's laws. Does a Christian philosophy result in a deterministic or legalistic understanding of reality? Not at all. And for two reasons.

First, our so-called scientific laws are not to be confused with God's law for creation. Scientific laws are theoretical constructions attempting to account for the lawfulness of creation. They are best understood as provisional theoretical approximations of how God orders the creation, and thus they should be held tentatively. For example, while the lawlike, predictable, reliable reality we all experience as gravity is constant, Newton's "law" of gravity came and went.

Second, we must distinguish God's order for the creation from the actual, concrete creation. While God's laws are universal, creation itself bursts with uniqueness and individuality.

All responses to God's law are historical. This is the (overstated) insight of the humanities side of the debate. While God's law does order creational life, it leaves room, especially in human life, for differing responses. God's law for our cultural life is a *calling* to which we respond, not a deterministic force. Therefore, the human process of developing culture is a fallible attempt to bring into concrete actuality God's laws for our cultural life. God has, for example, ordained a universal principle of justice as the law for political activity, but this principle becomes formulated and culturally enacted in an actual legal structure. Such legal structures are better or worse attempts to implement God's law for political life in his creation.

Indeed, all cultural life consists of fallible instances of God's law. Artistic work, family life, school systems and businesses are all responses to God's call for creative nuancefulness, trothfulness, nurture and stewardship respectively. These are the norms which must characterize the particular given structure. But no one instance of structure can stand as the true model, the right formulation. No particular, historically variable model of, say, the state (for example, the modern, liberal democratic model), or the family (for example, the twentieth-century nuclear model), or even a particular form of musical expression (for example, pretwentieth-century tonality) should every be absolutized. It should never imply that no other model or form could be obedient to God's word for aspects of creational life. In different historical and cultural situations, different responses may be both more appropriate and more obedient.

Recognizing that responses to creational law are always historically conditioned is a natural consequence of the distinction (made in chapter five) between structure and direction. While there is one structure of the creation (God's abiding, ordering and directing word), there are two possible *directions* in response (obedience or disobedience).

Nuclear fission, for example, is a possibility that God structured into creation, but the Christian technologist (and citizen) must ask, What spiritual direction is evident in our culture's nuclear technology? Because in our present culture such technology functions as a disobedient response to God's norms, we would call for a moratorium on it. We don't mean to encourage a back-to-nature romanticism which views such technology as inherently evil. But nuclear technology appears to serve both the ideology of militarism and the false gods of scientism, technicism and economism.

Reductionism versus Multidimensionality
The fact that the biblical world view often focuses on idolatry as the

root of creational misdirectedness gives rise to the third element of a Christian academic perspective. Not only must we reject scientism and grapple with God's order for creation, but we must also account for the multidimensionality of life.

In scholarship, multidimensionality is obscured by reductionism. Far more than a mere theoretical misconception, reductionism ultimately amounts to idol worship. When something in creation is not allowed to stand in its own creational integrity, but is rather consistently reduced to or explained in terms of something else, then a form of idolatry is lurking nearby.

Donald MacKay calls reductionism "nothing-buttery" because it always shortsightedly claims that something is "nothing-but" one of its constitutive elements.[4] For example, human consciousness is nothing but a series of complex physical-chemical interactions in the brain. Or, ethical values are nothing but emotional predispositions to, or means of, greater material utility. Or, the family is reduced to an economic unit, and society to a mechanism of human evolution.

Consider how even religion has been reduced to one element or another over the years. Freud with his theories of neurotic projection reduced religion to the emotional life. Marx (recall his notion of the opiate of the masses) reduced it to an element of economic life. Classical liberalism saw religion as a mode of social life. For Ritschl's neo-Kantian theology it was a system of values. Locke's rationalism (and much contemporary evangelical "propositionalism") reduced faith to a logical system. Each of these theories has some validity, for creation is truly multidimensional. Human religious life does include psychological, social, ethical and logical dimensions.[5] We err, however, if we reduce it to any one of these dimensions.

A philosophical question posed for Christians in any field of study is this: On what basis do we judge a position to be reductionistic? The only way we can truly discern reductionism is if we have some notion of irreducibles. And the notion of irreducibles depends on a theoretical account of the multidimensionality of life.

Herman Dooyeweerd's theory of the "modal aspects of reality" is such an account. Dooyeweerd explains multidimensionality not in terms of different kinds of creatures but in terms of *how* creatures operate, the *ways* they function. It is usually at this level that reductionism occurs.[6]

For example, although few people are prone to confusing a brain with a rock, many articulate and erudite scholars have argued that the functioning of the brain is nothing but a process of physical-chemical interactions. This does not reduce one particular thing to another; it reduces the many ways a particular thing in creation (the brain) functions to one of its constitutive functions (physical-chemical interactions). To guard against such reductionism, we need a formulation of the irreducible ways, modes, aspects or dimensions of creaturely functioning.

While we will not attempt such a full-scale formulation here, notice how the act of reading this book illustrates multidimensionality. The most obvious thing about a book is that it is written: it manifests a *lingual* dimension. But sermons are also written, and this book is not primarily a sermon. It is another kind of writing; it is (especially in this chapter) *theoretical* or *analytical* writing. Both the theoretical and lingual modalities (dimensions) play an important and interrelated role in the writing and reading of this book. Indeed, the book will be judged partially on whether it has been lingually clear and theoretically consistent.

Yet the reference to a sermon is still relevant because this book presupposes a certain *confessional* starting point which includes a commitment to biblical revelation and its relevance to all of life. Both of us authors have tried to illustrate how that revelation speaks to all of life, including scholarship. If we did not actually hold such convictions, there would be something unethical about our text. This then is another dimension—the *ethical*.

Other aspects could be noted as well. Consider the closely related *economic* and *legal* dimensions. The authors and publisher drew up a legal contract which included arrangements concerning the financial aspects of producing and selling a book. There is also an important *formative* aspect. We have attempted to provide an educational service to readers as they develop a Christian cultural vision and philosophical framework. Hence our subtitle "Shaping a Christian World View." Our language also has an *aesthetic* dimension insofar as it demonstrates a certain style of writing. And the fact that the book is coauthored and written in community with a number of other people discloses a *social* dimension to the book, as does its intention to interact with readers and encourage their communal interaction for mutual growth.

An *emotional* side comes in as well. Readers may be excited, intrigued or angered by what we have written. And, of course, emotions are related to a *physical-chemical* dimension; if a reader is angry, certain chemicals will interact in him or her in certain ways. Indeed, if it is late at night and the reader's energy level is low, then he or she may have difficulty in maintaining a high level of concentration.

So even the simple act of reading a book displays a diversity of aspects or dimensions. Of course, our list is not necessarily exhaustive, but it does give a sense of what a multidimensional analysis would look like. What is important is that such aspects are irreducible. One level or dimension of functioning can never be explained away or reduced to another without doing injustice to the multidimensionality of creation. A reader's anger or excitement has a physical-chemical side to it, but the psychic or emotional dimension is not reducible to its physical-chemical basis. Similarly, the book has a legitimate economic dimension, but its purpose should not be reduced to a business venture. In either case the integrity of the book, reader and authors is sacrificed.

Reductionism is an alluring temptation in scholarship precisely because the diverse modes of creaturely functioning are so coherent, interrelated and interdependent. All of the irreducible aspects can be found functioning in one way or another in all creaturely entities. For someone seeking an ultimate principle of explanation for broad areas of reality, the discovery that one particular modality or dimension is displayed in every entity and event would be very appealing. This person might use such alluring evidence to conclude that this modal aspect will work as an ultimate explanatory principle. The temptation is strongest for those who reject the Creator and must find such an explanatory principle immanent in the creation. Christian scholars, in contrast, find an ultimate principle in God's creating and sustaining word.

The temptation to reductionism is inherent in the nature of scientific knowledge itself. Sociologist Alan Storkey comments, "It is in the nature of a science that it abstracts from the full complexity of reality and analyzes in a particular way." Thus the botanist, physicist, philosopher, chemist and economist all study the same tree, but each respectively in terms of its biological, physical, ontological, chemical and economic dimensions. But it is imperative to note, says Storkey, that "no one analysis can claim to be the definitive one, for the process of abstraction from reality means that scientific knowledge is a partial and limited form of understanding."[7] Since, however, the academic world has absolutized science into scientism, and has elevated abstract thought as a model for all true knowledge, it is no wonder that various competing reductionisms are rampant.

In one sense, reductionism occurs when the law for one aspect of creaturely life is taken to be the law for another. Christian chemists, therefore, will analyze God's lawful structure for chemical functioning in the creation. Their analysis will also look at how chemical functions relate to biotic and psychological aspects, and it will resist reducing such aspects to chemistry. Similarly, political theorists will investigate the functionings of the state in terms of God's call for justice, and they will reduce the state to neither a mere organization of power nor a handmaiden of the economic sector. And although musicologists or composers may legitimately investigate the physical-acoustical, mathematical and psychological aspects of music, they will not lose sight of the fact that music is primarily an aesthetic expression of human creativity.

In chapter ten, our hypothetical business executive and doctor asked how they alone could possibly be agents of cultural renewal. Perhaps our hypothetical chemists, political theorists and musicologists could now be asking, "How can I alone withstand the idolatry of the academy, begin to discern God's law for my discipline, see how my field needs to be guarded against reductionism and also place my own scientific work in the context of the multidimensionality of reality?" To repeat, one person alone can do nothing. A Christian academic witness must be communal. So let us now briefly consider some practical ways Christians can help each other to develop a Christian perspective and witness in scholarship.[8]

Communal Christian Scholarship

Christ calls us to submit everything in our lives, including our studies, to his lordship. And we must submit not just individually, but also communally. Christian students should shun the competitive individualism of a job-oriented education and begin to struggle *together* to study in a way that reflects ultimate allegiance to Christ.

If a Christian perspective in scholarship is antireductionistic and attempts to honor the complex multidimensionality of God's creation, then Christian academic studies must be self-consciously interdisciplinary. True knowledge requires the integration of the particular insights of limited disciplines into a whole, integral picture. However, such wholistic knowledge is seldom found in the secular, specialized and dis-integrated university. Also, because integrated knowing requires a commonality of world view, which the university lacks, Christians will usually have to overcome this fragmentation of knowledge in other contexts than the classroom.

Christians in various disciplines need to help each other perceive the coherence and interrelatedness of the creation. One way they could do this, for instance, would be to foster study and discussion groups on campus. Perhaps these groups could be formed around various disciplines. In this context they could work together to develop a Christian perspective in that field and relate their work to other disciplines. They might write a paper together, or individual papers, on the topic of integration for a suitable course. This would be especially relevant in courses which deal with the "philosophy of" a discipline (for example, literary criticism, philosophy of science, philosophy of education, and political philosophy).

In courses that are not overtly philosophical, Christians should struggle together to ascertain the philosophical and world view perspective which is foundational to the way in which the professor (and textbook) present the material. We all know that the most effective way to learn is not through passive listening but through questions and dialog. We should not be afraid to have our world view clearly disclosed and opened to challenge. We should, however, be careful that our comments and questions do not needlessly alienate any professor or fellow student.

Christian students should also seek out Christian professors who have attempted to do their scholarship Christianly.[9] They could sponsor public debates and dialogs between Christian and non-Christian faculty members or guest scholars. Contrasting perspectives in various disciplines on assorted topics could thus be investigated. Although such events have an evangelistic effect, they are also ways for Christians to learn from non-Christians. Often, in fact, non-Christians have opened up the creation with theoretical insight while Christians have either hung on to worn-out ideas (how the church related to Galileo, for example) or have been unconcerned about such scientific insight because of their dualistic world view.

In the last few years we have witnessed an encouraging "renaissance" in the Christian community's approach to scholarship. As a result Christian students have available many books on Christianity and scholarship; they need to read these if they are seeking a Christian perspective in their studies. We have compiled for the appendix to this book a list of some of these resources. Communal study of such books will necessarily add to a student's workload, but Christian students will have to make such sacrifices. Perhaps students should even consider taking an extra year of study so that sufficient time is allowed to get a true education, rather than mere specialized training.

To be in community with one another means to be dependent on and subject to each other. As a result we should seek the counsel of brothers and sisters as we attempt to serve the Lord in our studies; we need to be open to each other's questions, concerns and perspectives.

At its root, scholarship is a particular response to the cultural mandate to till and keep the creational garden. As that task required the cohumanity of man and woman, so also the task of theoretically opening up and disclosing the creation is a communal task. In a fallen situation that task is redemptive. By doing scholarship rooted in a biblically inspired philosophical framework, we bear witness to the Creator and to his Son, Jesus Christ—the Word made flesh. Such scholarship gives hope for a renewed Christian academic presence, which in turn spreads shalom throughout our culture.

Notes

Chapter 1: World View and Culture

[1]*The Four Families,* National Film Board, 1959 (written and produced by Ian McNeil).

[2]Arnold H. DeGraaff, Jean Olthuis and Anne Tuininga, *Japan: A Way of Life* (Toronto: Joy in Learning Curriculum Development and Training Centre, 1980), p. 145.

[3]Ibid., p. 64.

[4]Ibid., p. 62.

[5]Quoted in Mel Watkins, ed., *Dene Nation: The Colony Within* (Toronto: Univ. of Toronto Press, 1977), p. 10.

[6]*Northern Frontier, Northern Homeland: The Report of the Mackenzie Valley Pipeline Inquiry,* vol. 1 (Ottawa: Ministry of Supply and Services, Canada, 1977), p. 85; hereafter referred to as NF/NH.

[7]Quoted in NF/NH, p. 90.

[8]Watkins, *Dene Nation,* p. 15.

[9]NF/NH, p. 1.

[10]See Hugh McCullum and Karmel McCullum, *This Land Is Not for Sale* (Toronto: Anglican Book Centre, 1975), p. 16.

[11]E. F. Schumacher, *Small Is Beautiful: A Study of Economics As If People Mattered* (London: Abacus Books, 1974), p. 84.

[12]Ibid., pp. 10-11.

[13]Bob Goudzwaard, *Capitalism and Progress: A Diagnosis of Western Society,* trans. Josina Van Nuis Zylstra (Grand Rapids, Mich.: Eerdmans, 1979), p. 24.

[14]Robert Heilbroner, *The Worldly Philosophers,* 4th ed. (New York: Simon and Schuster, 1972), p. 25.

[15]Quoted in McCullum and McCullum, *This Land Is Not for Sale,* p. 24.

[16]These several quotations are from NF/NH, pp. 94-95. ("Dene" is pronounced De-*nay*.)

[17]Quoted in McCullum and McCullum, *This Land Is Not for Sale,* p. 10.

[18]Ibid., p. 11.

[19]Watkins, *Dene Nation,* p. 8.

Chapter 2: Analyzing World Views

[1]For a helpful discussion of Paul's use of the terms *flesh* and *spirit* see Herman Ridderbos, *Paul: An Outline of His Theology,* trans. J. R. DeWitt (Grand Rapids, Mich.: Eerdmans, 1975), chap. 19.

[2]We are indebted to Dr. James Olthuis for much of the following material. We have gleaned his insights into visions of life primarily through seminars and unpublished manuscripts written at the Institute for Christian Studies in Toronto, Canada.

[3]Arnold H. DeGraaff, "Towards a New Anthropological Model," In J. Kraay and A. Tol, eds., *Hearing and Doing* (Toronto: Wedge, 1979), p. 101.

[4]Hendrik Hart, *The Challenge of Our Age* (Toronto: Wedge, 1974), p. 5.

[5]Benjamin L. Whorf, *Language, Thought and Reality,* ed. J. B. Carroll (Cambridge, Mass.: MIT, n.d.), p. vi.

[6]James W. Sire, *The Universe Next Door: A Basic World View Catalog* (Downers Grove, Ill.: InterVarsity Press, 1976), p. 16.

[7]On faith, see DeGraaff, "A New Anthropological Model," p. 99; and Alan Storkey, *A Christian Social Perspective* (Leicester, England: Inter-Varsity Press, 1976), pp. 15-17.

[8]Compare the kinds of questions listed by Storkey, ibid., p. 16, and by Sire, *Universe Next Door*, p. 18.

[9]See James W. Sire, "From the Bottom Up: World View Analysis as a Basis for Integration," in *Faith and Discipline* (Sterling, Kans.: Sterling College, 1980), pp. 18, 20. Arthur Holmes also has said that "the genesis of a worldview is at the prephilosophical level." *Contours of a Worldview* (Grand Rapids, Mich.: Eerdmans, 1983), p. 31.

[10]See Vincent Brummer, *Theology and Philosophical Inquiry: An Introduction* (Philadelphia: Westminster Press, 1982), p. 140.

[11]See Claude Ragan, "Perceptual Process and Christian Commitment," *Reformed Journal* 31, no. 5 (May 1981): 15-17.

[12]See DeGraaff et al., *Japan: A Way of Life*, pp. 211-13.

[13]See Bob Goudzwaard, *Idols of Our Time*, trans. Mark Vandervennen (Downers Grove, Ill.: InterVarsity Press, 1984).

[14]Compare Sire, *Universe Next Door*, p. 209.

[15]For example, see H. Richard Niebuhr, *Christ and Culture* (New York: Harper & Row, 1983).

Chapter 3: Based on Creation

[1]Note Francis Schaeffer's comment that "Christianity as a system does not begin with Christ as Savior, but with the infinite-personal God who created the world in the beginning and who made man significant in the flow of history." *Genesis in Space and Time: The Flow of Biblical History* (Downers Grove, Ill.: InterVarsity Press, 1972), p. 97.

[2]Clarence J. Glacken, in his monumental study on views of man and the world, affirms the importance of creation for the biblical world view. He states that Christianity is distinctively "a religion and a philosophy of creation," preoccupied with the Creator, the creation, and their relationships (p. 181). Note in particular the section in chapter 4, entitled "God, Man and Nature in Judeo-Christian Theology," *Traces on the Rhodian Shore: Nature and Culture in Western Thought from Ancient Times to the End of the Eighteenth Century* (Berkeley: Univ. of Calif. Press, 1976).

[3]See Genesis 1:3, 6, 9, 11, 14, 20, 24, 26. Note James Houston's comment in *I Believe in the Creator* (Grand Rapids, Mich.: Eerdmans, 1980), pp. 51, 272, 275, that *creatio per verbum* (creation by the word) is actually more basic than *creatio ex nihilo* (creation out of nothing). Walter Kaiser, Jr., in *Towards an Old Testament Theology* (Grand Rapids, Mich.: Zondervan, 1978), p. 74, points out that it is also an older formulation.

[4]The reference in Isaiah 55:10-11 is to God's *prophetic* word, which is so authoritative it guarantees the fulfillment. In Genesis 1 it is God's *creative* word. In both cases God's word has the same characteristics: it accomplishes his will.

[5]See Genesis 1:7, 9, 11, 15, 24. The ease with which God structures creation in Genesis is in direct contrast to other creation accounts from the ancient Near East, of which the Babylonian-Sumerian *Enuma Elish* is perhaps the most famous. In the *Enuma Elish*, for example, creation is accomplished through a tremendous battle. The account is filled with warring gods and monsters, and out of the climactic battle between Marduk

(the rising sun-god) and Tiamat (the primeval waters) the world is created. Genesis, however, portrays God as absolutely sovereign; he only needs to speak and his creation obeys. See Barbara C. Sproul, *Primal Myths: Creating the World* (San Francisco: Harper & Row, 1979) for an extensive anthology of creation accounts, not only from the Near East, but from all major civilizations and cultures. See pp. 91-113 for the *Enuma Elish.* Paul Ricoeur's *The Symbolism of Evil,* trans. E. Buchanan (Boston: Beacon Press, 1969), pt. 2, chaps. 1 and 3, also compares the Babylonian world view with the Hebrew.

[6]See Genesis 1:4, 10, 12, 18, 21, 25, 31. This unequivocal affirmation of the intrinsic goodness of created reality is unparalleled in all the accounts of origins that we have thus far investigated. All other creation accounts, whether tribal or national mythologies, or the statements of modern philosophically oriented thinkers regarding origins, inevitably *begin* with the existence of evil in some form—unless they have been influenced by the Bible. It seems that because of human experience of the Fall, our attempt to construct a world view independent of biblical revelation will lead to the postulation of a flawed beginning, an initial ambiguity of good and evil.

[7]While the Scripture quotations throughout this book are taken from the New International Version (NIV) because of its general readability, we have sometimes brought the translation more in line with a literal reading. All such changes will be noted. One main adaptation that begins here, and which occurs in other quotations as well, is the rendering of the NIV "LORD" as "Yahweh," the personal, covenantal name for God in the Old Testament (see Ex 3:13-15 and 6:2-4). Since we are trying to recapture the biblical world view, it is only appropriate that we use the more literal "Yahweh" in these contexts.

[8]This teaching is also found in the New Testament (NT) in Hebrews 11:3 and 2 Peter 3:5 and 7, and it is the underlying idea of John 1:1-3, where Christ is said to be the Word by whom God made the universe. It is also the basis of Hebrews 1:1-3, which states that the world was created through Christ and that he upholds it by *his* word. The NT teaching on this issue, however, takes us a step further, and this new understanding cannot simply be presupposed in the OT references. The literary contexts are essential here.

[9]We have departed from the NIV in this passage by substituting the more literal "utters his voice" (cf. RSV, NASB) for the NIV "thunders," which, although not incorrect, tends to overlook the connection with the idea of creation by the word.

[10]Note that the NIV "empty" is translated as "a chaos" in the RSV and as "a waste land" in the NASB. The idea is that of an unformed (not a deformed) mass.

[11]A cursory survey turned up approximately forty biblical references to the earth or the world's being "founded" or "established." One quarter of these are found in the NT. See for example Mt 13:35; Lk 11:50; Jn 17:24; Eph 1:4; Heb 9:26.

[12]Deism was a transitional philosophy between Christian theism and atheism, which flourished in the eighteenth century. Deism postulated a God, but a God not particularly involved in the universe—an absentee Creator who set the world in motion but then retired from view. For a good introduction to the deistic world view see Sire, *Universe Next Door,* pp. 44-56.

[13]Other passages that speak of God's relationship with creation as covenantal are Jer 31:35-37; Ezek 34:23-31 and Hos 2:18. See also the glowing description of God's care for his

world in Ps 65:9-13.

[14]For an excellent account of the historical debates, see G. C. Berkouwer, *Man: The Image of God*, trans. D. Jellema (Grand Rapids, Mich.: Eerdmans, 1962), esp. chap. 2. In our discussion of the meaning of the image which follows, we have omitted on the one hand the Mormon interpretation of mankind as the image of a literal, physical, flesh-and-bones god (a divinized human being), and on the other hand the supposed distinction between "image" and "likeness" in Genesis 1:26. Biblical scholarship has amply shown such a distinction to be illusory; the terms are synonymous.

[15]Here are some helpful studies on the image of God which have contributed to our interpretation: Ranald Macaulay and Jerram Barrs, *Being Human: The Nature of Spiritual Experience* (Downers Grove, Ill.: InterVarsity Press, 1978); Berkouwer, *Man: The Image of God;* Meredith G. Kline, *Images of the Spirit* (Grand Rapids, Mich.: Baker Book House, 1980); P. Schrotenboer, *Man in God's World: The Biblical Idea of Office* (Toronto: Wedge, 1972). See also H. Fernhout, "Man: The Image and Glory of God" (mimeographed, Toronto, A.A.C.S.) and K. L. McKay, "Creation," in *The New Bible Dictionary,* ed. J. D. Douglas et al. (London: Inter-Varsity Press, 1962).

[16]For a similar analysis of *culture* see Niebuhr, *Christ and Culture,* chap. 1; and J. F. Kavanaugh, *Following Christ in a Consumer Society: The Spirituality of Cultural Resistance* (Maryknoll, N.Y.: Orbis, 1981), pp. 55-62.

[17]See Derek Kidner, *Genesis: An Introduction and Commentary* (Downers Grove, Ill.: InterVarsity Press, 1967), pp. 23-24, for a discussion of the significance of the *toledoth* structure of Genesis.

[18]As in Genesis 5:1; 10:1; 25:12; 36:1, 9.

[19]See Genesis 2:4; 6:9; 11:10, 27; 25:19; 37:2.

[20]A similar analogy is found in a number of parables that Jesus told to illustrate the kingdom of God. God is either a master hiring servants or a landowner renting out his land to tenant farmers. (See for example Mt 20:1-16; 24:42-51; Lk 19:11-27; 20:9-18.) The Genesis mandate seems to have played a major role in Jesus' thinking.

Chapter 4: Acknowledging the Fall

[1]The first two references are found in the Jacob narratives, Genesis 31:19 ("household gods") and Genesis 35:2, 4 ("foreign gods").

[2]Although a number of Hebrew words translate as "image" in the Old Testament, human beings are referred to as the *selem* of God in Genesis 1:26-27; 5:1; and 9:6. This word is also used in reference to idols in Numbers 33:52; 2 Kings 11:18; 2 Chronicles 23:17; Ezekiel 7:20; 16:17; and Amos 5:26. Walter Kaiser in *Towards an Old Testament Theology,* p. 76, translates *selem* as "carved or hewn statue or copy."

[3]See Berkouwer, *Man: The Image of God,* pp. 67-118; also the article "Image" by Ralph P. Martin in *The New International Dictionary of New Testament Theology,* vol 2, ed. Colin Brown (Grand Rapids, Mich.: Zondervan, 1976), esp. p. 287.

[4]In light of the above discussion we would take issue with Francis Schaeffer's recent and influential interpretation of the image of God in man. He takes the term to mean simply our humanity—or, to be more precise, our "personality," our unique nature as human persons. See *The God Who Is There* (Downers Grove, Ill.: InterVarsity Press, 1968), p. 87; *Genesis in Space and Time,* p. 47; and also Thomas V. Morris, *Francis Schaeffer's Apologetics: A Critique* (Chicago: Moody Press, 1976), p. 26.

While Schaeffer is quite right in connecting our humanity with the image of God (since it is human beings who are in the image), this position needs two important qualifications. First, the image of God is not our humanity in the sense of our "person-hood" narrowly construed, for it also includes our very bodily existence. Second, the image refers not simply to our human nature but (as Macaulay and Barrs indicate in *Being Human,* chap. 1) to normative humanness, our attempts to live up to God's stan-dards in all that we do. Moreover we must view this humanness as our fulfillment of the cultural mandate (a point not emphasized by Macaulay and Barrs). Our humanity and the image of God, therefore, are linked but cannot be unqualifiedly identified. As Meredith Kline points out in *Images of the Spirit,* p. 33, they are "not simple equivalents."
[5]We have departed from the NIV here by substituting the more accurate word *image* for the looser term *idol* in verse 4.
[6]For an illuminating biblical-theological analysis of the covenant in the OT, see Meredith G. Kline, *The Structure of Biblical Authority,* rev. ed. (Grand Rapids, Mich.: Eerdmans, 1975).
[7]See Mt 12:24; Mk 3:22; Lk 11:15; Jn 12:31; 14:30; 16:11; see also Eph 2:2.
[8]C. S. Lewis, "Peace Proposals for Brother Every and Mr. Bethell," *Christian Reflections,* ed. Walter Hooper (Glasgow: Collins, Fount Paperbacks, 1981), p. 52.

Chapter 5: Transformed by Redemption
[1]*Redemptive history* as a technical, theological term is based on the German *Heilsgeschichte,* which means literally "holy history." It is sometimes translated as "salvation history." The concept of *Heilsgeschichte* is associated with theologians such as Gerhard von Rad, *Old Testament Theology,* 2 vols. (New York: Harper & Row, 1962-66); G. Ernest Wright, *God Who Acts: Biblical Theology as Recital* (London: S.P.C.K., 1952); and Oscar Cull-mann, *Christ and Time: The Primitive Christian Conception of Time and History,* trans. Floyd U. Filson, rev. ed. (Philadelphia: Westminster Press, 1964). See Steven H. Travis, *Christian Hope and the Future* (Downers Grove, Ill.: InterVarsity Press, 1980), pp. 83-89.
[2]For an excellent, brief exposition of Old Testament covenant history, which is sensitive to the unity of Scripture and the biblical world view, see Don Sinnema, *Reclaiming the Land: A Study of the Book of Joshua,* teacher and study-group edition (Toronto: Curricu-lum Development Centre, 1977), pp. 4ff. For a good, popular treatment of the entire Bible from a covenantal perspective, see S. G. De Graff, *Promise and Deliverance,* 4 vols. (St. Catherines, Ontario: Paideia Press, 1977-82).
[3]Compare also the narrowed, more exclusive covenant sign of circumcision in the Abra-hamic covenant with the universal rainbow, the sign of the Noahic covenant.
[4]See Sinnema, *Reclaiming the Land,* for an analysis of the conquest of Canaan in light of this discussion.
[5]For an excellent, thorough study of the kingdom of God in the preaching of Jesus, see Herman Ridderbos, *The Coming of the Kingdom* (Philadelphia: Presbyterian and Re-formed, 1962). Another scholarly, though more accessible, work is chapter 2 of G. E. Ladd, *The Pattern of New Testament Truth* (Grand Rapids, Mich.: Eerdmans, 1968), on the synoptic pattern. Ladd does a brilliant job of relating the theme of the kingdom of God to other central themes in the rest of the New Testament.
[6]The background imagery is drawn both from the exodus (the new Moses who will lead the people to freedom) and the teachings in Leviticus 25 concerning the year of

jubilee, when people regain their creational inheritance.

[7]See Ridderbos, *Coming of the Kingdom,* pp. 211-32. Also helpful is his article "The Biblical Message of Reconciliation" in *Studies in Scripture and Its Authority* (Grand Rapids, Mich.: Eerdmans, 1972).

[8]We would suggest that the fire of judgment in 2 Peter 3 is to be understood as a "cleansing" fire which reveals the truth and goodness of creation. The NIV reads in verse 10, "The earth and everything in it will be laid bare."

[9]1 John 3:8 states that "the reason the Son of God appeared was to destroy the devil's work."

[10]For a presentation (including a rebuttal) of postmillennialism, see Robert G. Clouse, ed., *The Meaning of the Millennium: Four Views* (Downers Grove, Ill.: InterVarsity Press, 1977), pp. 117-52.

[11]1 Corinthians 5:6-8; Matthew 13:5-12 (see also Mark 8:15 and Luke 12:1); and Galatians 5:9 refer to sin as leaven.

[12]The D-day/V-day imagery is taken from Cullmann, *Christ and Time,* p. 84. See Ladd, *Pattern of New Testament Truth,* p. 50.

[13]This is not to suggest a doctrine of universal salvation, for the Bible is clear on the fact of judgment. We are, however, addressing another point; namely, as Francis Schaeffer puts it in *Art and the Bible: Two Essays* (Downers Grove, Ill.: InterVarsity Press, 1973), p. 7, that "in Christ the whole man is redeemed." Salvation does not simply apply to a part of life, but to the *whole* of it. Neither art nor sexuality nor politics is irredeemable. God will purify his creation of all sin. Therefore, unholy art will have no part in the kingdom, neither will prostitution, nor any form of illegitimate sexuality, nor corrupt political systems. The problem is that we do not know just how much of creation will have to be transformed in order to be purified. Even Paul professed a great degree of ignorance regarding the new creation (1 Cor 2:9). An interesting indication, however, is found in Revelation 21, where John mentions that in the new heaven and earth there will be nations and kings, and the "glory and honor" of the nations will be brought into the New Jerusalem (21:1, 24, 26).

[14]Note that other titles for Christ also reflect this ambiguity. For example, "Son of God" can be taken as referring both to Christ's humanity (as we are also sons and daughters of God) and to his unique Sonship (the "only begotten" Son). Further, "son of man," a common Jewish idiom for a human being (see Ps 8:4 and Ezek 2:1, 3, 6, etc.), also has reference to the divine Messiah figure "like a son of man" in Daniel's apocalyptic vision (7:13-14).

[15]See 1 Cor 3:16-17; 6:19; 2 Cor 6:16; Eph 2:19-22; 1 Pet 2:4-5; compare Rev 21:2-3, 9-14.

[16]Note the significant title of the very good book by Ranald Macaulay and Jerram Barrs, *Being Human: The Nature of Spiritual Experience.* This title solidly reflects the biblical world view.

[17]See 2 Tim 2:12; Rev 5:10; 20:4, 6. Compare the passages that speak of our judging the world, like Lk 22:30; 1 Cor 6:2; and Rev 20:4.

[18]For this illustration we are indebted to our colleague Al Wolters, formerly of the Institute for Christian Studies.

Chapter 6: The Problem of Dualism

[1]Jim Wallis, "Rebuilding the Church," *Sojourners* 9, no. 1 (January 1980): 10.

[2]Compare Acts 17:6. Perhaps the problem is even more acute when we use the word *evangelical*. Why is the radical power of the "evangel" so often lacking in our lives as evangelicals? Speaking specifically of American evangelicalism, Os Guinness has observed that the "spirituality" of the American evangelical community is "privately engaging but socially irrelevant." "Thus it has no historical-cultural impact in terms of the Kingdom of God reaching out into society" ("The American Church Faces the 80's: A Moment Not to Be Missed," *Radix* 13, no. 6 [May/June 1982]: 10).

[3]Bernard Zylstra says that "the Christian religion, having lost the wide scope of a God-centred walk of life, narrowed down to man-centred soul salvation, has become for many the moral justification for nationalism, the American way of life, and all that it stands for in the world today" ("Thy Word Our Life," In *Will All the King's Men, . . .* [Toronto: Wedge, 1972], p. 201).

[4]Compare Howard Snyder's comment: "An evangelism which focuses exclusively on souls or on an otherworldly transaction which makes no real difference here and now is unfaithful to the gospel" (*The Community of the King* [Downers Grove, Ill.: InterVarsity Press, 1977], p. 102).

[5]"Must the Church Become Secular?" in *Out of Concern for the Church* (Toronto: Wedge, 1970), p. 117. Olthuis says further, "The most disheartening feature of this painful state of affairs is the fact that the Body of Christ—with few exceptions—does not recognize these chains when they clang and rattle. She does not see that it is her own way-of-thinking that has at the ouset compromised the Gospel" (p. 122).

[6]John R. W. Stott, *Christian Mission in the Modern World* (Downers Grove, Ill.: Inter-Varsity Press, 1975), p. 31.

[7]Compare Brian Walsh, "How to Think Your Way through College," *HIS* (November 1983).

[8]Quoted by E. Vanderkloet, "Why Work Anyway?" in *Labour of Love: Essays on Work* (Toronto: Wedge, 1980), p. 21.

[9]Paul Marshall, "Vocation, Work and Jobs," in *Labour of Love,* p. 4.

[10]Ibid., p. 5.

[11]Ibid., p. 7.

[12]See Thomas Aquinas, *Summa Theologiae* 2. 2. 179.1-2; 2. 2. 181.1-4; 2. 2. 182.1-2.

[13]Marshall, "Vocation, Work and Jobs," p. 8.

[14]Niebuhr, *Christ and Culture,* chaps. 2, 4, 5.

[15]Of course, our descriptions here have somewhat the character of caricature in order to communicate the functioning of these different perspectives.

[16]Niebuhr also refers to two other options, namely, "Christ of culture" and "Christ transforms culture." The first simply identifies Christianity uncritically with the best of human culture. This classical "liberalism" has no biblical basis whatsoever and will not be dealt with in this book. The second option, which Niebuhr identifies with Augustine and the views of F. D. Maurice, is precisely the perspective of this book. The problem, however, is that Augustine cannot always be interpreted consistently in a "Christ transforms culture" way and F. D. Maurice can't either. We suggested in chapter three that the biblical perspective is the transformist one. We also find that the tradition of Calvin carries this perspective into our own times in a way which is most sensitive and faithful to the biblical world view.

[17]Macaulay and Barrs, *Being Human*, p. 54. See also Herman Ridderbos, *Paul: An Outline of His Theology*, trans. J. R. DeWitt (Grand Rapids, Mich.: Eerdmans, 1975), pp. 91-93.

[18]Ibid., p. 76.

[19]Compare Douglas Webster, *Christian Living in a Pagan Culture* (Wheaton: Tyndale House, 1980), pp. 18, 95, 101, 126, 136. For a critique of this "soft dualism" see Brian Walsh's review of Webster in *Radix* 13, no. 3 (November/December 1981): 28-29.

[20]See for example Webster, *Christian Living*, p. 29.

[21]Snyder, *Community of the King*, p. 22. Compare Stott, *Christian Mission*, pp. 23-24.

[22]Macaulay and Barrs say, "It is not a nonhuman or suprahuman experience which we will enjoy in the future with our resurrected bodies. It is simply a human experience set free at last from the shackles of sin" (*Being Human*, p. 25). Dualism always makes us feel uncomfortable with our humanness, not at home in God's creation.

[23]See Revelation 21 where the New Jerusalem comes down to earth, rather than Christians going up to heaven. Biblical eschatology is creational eschatology. Indeed, there is not one biblical reference to Christians living eternally in heaven.

Chapter 7: The Development of Dualism

[1]See J. L. Gonzalez, *A History of Christian Thought* (Nashville: Abingdon Press, 1970), 1:47; Jack Rogers and Donald McKim, *The Authority and Interpretation of the Bible: An Historical Approach* (New York: Harper & Row, 1979), p. 7; and David Knowles, *The Evolution of Medieval Thought* (New York: Random House, 1962), p. 17.

[2]Francis Schaeffer, *Escape from Reason* (Downers Grove, Ill.: InterVarsity Press, 1968), p. 17.

[3]Rogers and McKim, *Authority and Interpretation*, p. 5.

[4]Gonzalez, *History of Christian Thought*, p. 48.

[5]For a helpful analysis of the development of the form/matter dualism in Greek philosophy see Herman Dooyeweerd, *Roots of Western Culture: Pagan, Secular, and Christian Options*, trans. J. Kraay (Toronto: Wedge, 1979), pp. 15-22, 111-13.

[6]Gonzalez, *History of Christian Thought*, p. 49. Compare Macaulay and Barrs, *Being Human*, pp. 38-42.

[7]David Knowles says that Plato is the father of all those "who find the true life of the human spirit in an upward striving towards the divine" (*Evolution of Medieval Thought*, p. 11).

[8]*Phaedo*, trans. P. J. Church (New York: Bobbs Merrill, 1951), p. 30 (80).

[9]Ibid., pp. 33 (82 and 83), 30 (80) and 12 (66).

[10]Compare Gonzalez, *History of Christian Thought*, p. 120.

[11]See H. Evan Runner, *The Christian and the World* (Toronto: Association for the Advancement of Christian Scholarship), p. 7.

[12]See also Knowles, *Evolution of Medieval Thought*, p. 23; Macaulay and Barrs, *Being Human*, p. 43.

[13]Knowles, *Evolution of Medieval Thought*, p. 38.

[14]A. H. Armstrong, *An Introduction to Ancient Philosophy* (London: Methuen, 1965), p. 178. Knowles goes so far as to say that if the Scriptures gave no clear direction on any issue, Augustine "accepted from the *Timaeus* and *Meno* of Plato and the *Enneads* of Plotinus the explanations they gave of the intellectual problems that engaged his atten-

NOTES

tion" (*Evolution of Medieval Thought*, p. 36).

15 Augustine, *City of God* (trans. M. Dods), 22.24. Compare Dooyeweerd, *Roots of Western Culture*, p. 115. Knowles says that for Augustine "as for Plato, the soul is a complete spiritual entity 'using' a body" (*Evolution of Medieval Thought*, p. 40).

16 Augustine, *City of God* 14.16-26.

17 Quoted by A. A. Maurer, *Medieval Philosophy* (New York: Random House, 1962), p. 8.

18 See Dooyeweerd, *Roots of Western Culture*, p. 122.

19 See Bob Goudzwaard, *Capitalism and Progress*, pp. 2, 6; and Heilbroner, *Worldly Philosophers*, pp. 6-27.

20 See Knowles, *Evolution of Medieval Thought*, p. 257.

21 Dooyeweerd, *Roots of Western Civilization*, p. 117. Compare Dooyeweerd's *In the Twilight of Western Thought* (Philadelphia, Pa.: Presbyterian and Reformed, 1960), pp. 191-93.

22 Ibid.

23 *The Imitation of Christ* is a Christian devotional book from the late Middle Ages which focuses on a fundamental dualism: the "within" (the soul, where God and Christ dwell) and the "without" (the natural world). Considerably more extreme than either Augustine or Aquinas, the author counsels the reader to "give up this worthless world" and to learn "indifference to all that lies outside" in order to find God (p. 83). He views Christ as one who teaches us "to spurn the things of earth, and to loathe what is temporal" (p. 176). Why? "When you turn your eyes toward created things you lose the vision of the Creator" (p. 175). Instead we are to pursue the path of the inner life and thus attain purification from the corrupting influence of external nature. The main impediment to the spiritual life is therefore to think "anything of value other than the one immeasurable, eternal Good. Whatever is not God is nothing, and must be considered nothing" (p. 160).

The page numbers we have given are from Thomas à Kempis, *The Imitation of Christ*, trans. Betty I. Knott (London: Collins, 1963). The dust jacket of this edition claims: "After the Bible, this is perhaps the most widely read book in the world. Since it was written, early in the fifteenth century, thousands of editions and translations have appeared." No wonder we find the prevalence of dualism in the modern church!

24 Jacques Monod, *Chance and Necessity: An Essay on the Natural Philosophy of Modern Biology*, trans. Austryn Wainhouse (New York: Random House, 1972), p. 174.

25 Schaeffer, *Escape from Reason*, p. 13. Schaeffer's discussion of the medieval nature/grace scheme (as well as his later discussion of the modern humanistic freedom/matter tension) is based on the analyses of Herman Dooyeweerd. See chaps. 5-7 of Dooyeweerd's *Roots of Western Culture*, a book which originally appeared in Dutch as a series of newspaper articles between 1945 and 1948.

26 Bernard Zylstra, "Modernity and the American Empire," *International Reformed Bulletin*, no. 68/29 (First-Second Quarter, 1971): 5-6.

Chapter 8: The Rise of the Secular World View

1 For a most helpful discussion of secularization and the resulting cultural captivity of the church, see Os Guinness, *The Gravedigger File: Papers on the Subversion of the Modern Church* (Downers Grove, Ill.: InterVarsity Press, 1983).

2 Giovanni Pico della Mirandola, *Oration on the Dignity of Man*, trans. A. Robert Caponigri

(Chicago: Henry Regnery Co., 1965), pp. 7-8.

[3]Although many modern thinkers have taken their inspiration from Pico's *Oration,* it is unclear to what extent Pico himself was consistently motivated by the spirit of modernity. The rest of the *Oration,* for example, has a distinctly medieval and mystical orientation. The purpose of human freedom is to aspire after God and so to attain heavenly rest and peace. See S. Dresden, *Humanism in the Renaissance,* trans. Margaret King (New York: McGraw Hill, 1968), pp. 13-14. Nevertheless, Pico definitely proclaimed a variey of humanism that has had a formative influence on the Western world view.

[4]Dooyeweerd, *Roots of Western Culture,* p. 150; Dooyeweerd's emphasis.

[5]A good historical resource is Clarence J. Glacken, *Traces on the Rhodian Shore: Nature and Culture in Western Thought from Ancient Times to the End of the Eighteenth Century* (Berkeley: Univ. of Calif. Press, 1976). See esp. chap. 5.

[6]Francis Bacon, *Novum Organum* 2. 52, in *The New Organon and Related Writings,* ed. Fulton H. Anderson (New York: The Liberal Arts Press, 1960), p. 267.

[7]John Passmore, *Man's Responsibility for Nature: Ecological Problems and Western Traditions* (London: Gerald Duckworth, 1974), p. 19. For a good analysis of Western man's autonomous domination of nature, see chap. 1, "Man as Despot."

[8]Francis Bacon, "New Atlantis," in *Ideal Commonwealths,* ed. by Henry Morely (New York: Colonial Press, 1901; rev. ed.), p. 129.

[9]Bacon, *Novum Organum* 1. 129, in *New Organon and Related Writings,* pp. 118-19.

[10]Passmore, *Man's Responsibility for Nature,* p. 19; Passmore's emphasis.

[11]It is important not to overstate the case of Bacon's secular scientism. Frank E. Manuel and Fritzie P. Manuel, for example, in their *Utopian Thought in the Western World* (Cambridge: Belknap Press of Harvard Univ. Press, 1979) point out that one does violence to Bacon to lift his scientific utopia out of his moral and religious framework (pp. 259-60). They nevertheless admit that it is "hard to overestimate the central role of science" in his *New Atlantis,* where he describes his utopia as a society of "scientist-priests" and his world view as ambivalent on the science-religion issue (pp. 254, 260). Note also the following passage from a little-known early work of Bacon's *(The Masculine Birth of Time),* in which he addresses an imaginary disciple: "My dear, dear boy, what I purpose is to unite you with *things themselves* in a chaste, holy, and legal wedlock; and from this association you will secure an increase beyond all the hopes and prayers of ordinary marriages, to wit, a blessed race of Heroes or Supermen who will overcome the immeasurable helplessness and poverty of the human race, which cause it more destruction than all giants, monsters, or tyrants, and will make you peaceful, happy, prosperous, and secure" (quoted in *Utopian Thought,* p. 260).

[12]René Descartes, *Discourse on Method,* chap. 6, in *Essential Works of Descartes,* trans. Lowell Bair (New York: Bantam, 1961), p. 37.

[13]Richard Foster Jones, *Ancients and Moderns: A Study of the Rise of the Scientific Movement in Seventeenth Century England* (New York: Dover Publications, 1982), p. ix. The next two paragraphs are indebted to this historical study, esp. pp. ix-xi, 45-55, 233.

[14]Ibid., pp. 50-51, 60, 124, 155, 185, 233-34, 266.

[15]Ibid., p. 234. Cowley went on to compare Isaac Newton to Joshua, who did lead the people into the Promised Land.

[16]Ibid., pp. 185, 235; emphasis added.

[17]Ibid., p. ix.

[18]Passmore, *Man's Responsibility for Nature,* p. 21.

[19]Newton is a good example of one who combined a strong commitment to both experimentation and mathematical explanation. And it is his name that is usually associated with the "mechanistic world picture." We have, however, focused on the mechanism of Descartes rather than of Newton, because of Descartes' historical priority and philosophical influence. For an analysis of Newton, see J. Bronowski, *The Common Sense of Science* (Cambridge: Harvard Univ. Press, 1978), chaps. 2 and 3.

[20]Passmore, *Man's Responsibility for Nature,* p. 22. As is now probably clear, we have not attempted to give even a summary history of the scientific revolution. That is far beyond the scope of this book. We have simply highlighted certain "world-viewish" elements in Bacon and Descartes which have significantly contributed to the rise of modern science as well as the development of scien*tism* in the modern world view.

[21]See, for example, Schaeffer, *Escape from Reason,* pp. 30-32.

[22]See chap. 10 of this book on the important distinction between structure and rationality (or order and logical order).

[23]R. Hooykaas, *Religion and the Rise of Modern Science* (Grand Rapids, Mich.: Eerdmans, 1972), p. 85.

[24]See chap. 2, "The Development of a Voluntarist Theology of Creation," in Eugene M. Klaaren, *Religious Origins of Modern Science: Belief in Creation in Seventeenth-Century Thought* (Grand Rapids, Mich.: Eerdmans, 1977).

Chapter 9: The Gods of Our Age

[1]Os Guinness, *The Dust of Death* (Downers Grove, Ill.: InterVarsity Press, 1973), p. 15.

[2]Jeremy Rifkin (with Ted Howard), *The Emerging Order: God in the Age of Scarcity* (New York: G. P. Putnam's Sons, 1979), p. 27.

[3]Goudzwaard, *Capitalism and Progress,* pp. 57-59; Goudzwaard's emphasis.

[4]Jeremy Rifkin (with Ted Howard), *Entropy: A New World View* (New York: Viking Press, 1980), p. 17.

[5]Ibid.

[6]Quoted in James M. Houston, "Space, Time, and Authenticity," *Regent College Bulletin* (Fall 1980).

[7]*Technology: Abandon, Endure or Advance?* (Chicago, Ill.: Gould Inc., n.d.), pp. 5, 9, 12.

[8]Although we have not mentioned the feet of clay mixed with iron of Nebuchadnezzar's statue, the analogy could be pushed to suggest that these weak feet represent the uneasy synthesis of the Greek and Christian world views of the medieval period, which we discussed in chapter four. We would also hasten to add that we are using Daniel 2 *analogically* and are not claiming to be providing a modern *exegesis* of the text.

[9]Heilbroner, *Worldly Philosophers,* pp. 14, 24, 21, 20.

[10]Karl Polanyi, *The Great Transformation* (Boston: Beacon Press, 1957), p. 30.

[11]Quoted in Heilbroner, *Worldly Philosophers,* p. 21.

[12]John K. Galbraith, *The New Industrial State* (Boston: Houghton Mifflin Co., 1967), p. 164.

[13]Ronald Sider, *Rich Christians in an Age of Hunger,* rev. ed. (Downers Grove, Ill.: InterVarsity Press, 1984), p. 38.

[14]Bob Goudzwaard, *Aid for the Overdeveloped West* (Toronto: Wedge, 1975), p. 15.

[15]Walter Wink, "Unmasking the Powers: A Biblical View of Roman and American Economics," *Sojourners* 7, no. 10 (October 1978): 14.

[16]Bruce Cockburn, "Candy Man's Gone," from the album *The Trouble with Normal*, copyright 1983, Golden Mountain Music Corp.; emphasis added. Reprinted by permission.

[17]In *Essays in Persuasion* (New York: Harcourt, Brace and Co., 1932), p. 372.

[18]Ibid., p. 371.

[19]Langdon Gilkey, *Society and the Sacred: Toward a Theology of Culture in Decline* (New York: Crossroads), p. xi; our emphasis.

[20]Ibid., p. 3.

[21]Rifkin, *Emerging Order*, p. 69.

[22]Ibid., p. 212.

[23]See Ruben Nelson, "The Exhaustion of Liberalism," in *Through the 80's: Thinking Globally, Acting Locally*, ed. Frank Feather (Washington, D.C.: World Futures Society, 1980), p. 22.

[24]Martin Buber, *I and Thou*, trans. W. Kaufman (New York: Charles Scribner's Sons, 1970).

[25]Gilkey, *Society and the Sacred*, p. 82.

[26]See Goudzwaard, *Aid for the Overdeveloped West*, p. 63.

[27]Robert Heilbroner, *An Inquiry into the Human Prospect* (New York: W. W. Norton and Co., 1974), p. 20.

[28]Ibid., p. 83. For a similar analysis see Daniel Bell, *The Cultural Contradictions of Capitalism*, 2d ed. (London: Heineman, 1979) and Goudzwaard, *Capitalism and Progress*.

[29]For an intriguing analysis of the energy issue see Jeremy Rifkin (with Ted Howard), *Entropy: A New World View*. From a Christian perspective, "Citizens for Public Justice" (formerly known as the "Committee for Justice and Liberty") has done some of the best work. See John Olthuis's article, "On Peeling an Onion," *CJL Newsletter*, Fall 1970 (229 College St., Toronto, Ontario, M5T 1R4).

[30]Rifkin, *Emerging Order*, p. 94.

[31]There are, of course, always a few people who hold onto the faith as long as possible. Indeed, there are many futurists who fail to see the need for a major world view or cultural shift. Rather than speaking of limits, Frank Feather proclaims that the "potential of our collective brains is probably infinite" ("Transition to Harmonic Globalism," in *Through the 80's*, p. 7). At the same conference (of which this volume is the collected papers), Hermann Kahn and John Phelps express a similar optimism. We do well to quote them at some length:
> On the whole . . . this problem-prone, super-industrial period will be marked by rising living standards and less rather than more sacrifice. Eventually, almost all of the problems will be dealt with reasonably satisfactorily, so that at the end of the transition period, the true post-industrial society can emerge ("The Economic Future," p. 208).

Ruben Nelson's analysis seems to have more integrity: "The thought is occurring among more and more of us that our problem is not that we lack able administration, but that we have no common purpose, no vision to guide us as we venture into the wilderness" ("The Exhaustion of Liberalism," p. 27).

[32]Bell, *Cultural Contradictions of Capitalism*, pp. 29-30. When Bell and others speak of

"modernity" they are actually referring to what we have been calling the modern world view and the culture it has produced. For a Christian analysis and critique of Bell's book see Bernard Zylstra's "A Neoconservative Critique of Modernity: Daniel Bell's Appraisal," *Christian Scholar's Review* 7, no. 4 (1978).

³³Compare Bell, *Cultural Contradictions of Capitalism,* p. 166 and Rifkin, *The Emerging Order,* pp. 241, 269.

Chapter 10: A Christian Cultural Response

¹Robert Heilbroner describes "the outlook for what we may call 'Convulsive change'—change forced upon us by external events rather than by conscious choice, by catastrophe rather than by calculation." He continues, "Nature will provide the checks, if foresight and 'morality' do not" (*An Inquiry into the Human Prospect,* p. 132).

²The interrelation of abortion and the nuclear arms race was dealt with in *Sojourner,* November 1980.

³For a good discussion of a Christian response to the values education issue, see Tom Malcolm and Harry Fernhout, *Education and the Public Purpose* (Toronto: Curriculum Development Centre, 1979). The Curriculum Development Centre has also published curriculum materials for schools which are written from the perspective of a Christian philosophy of education.

⁴See Goudzwaard, *Capitalism and Progress,* pp. 187-88, and *Aid for the Overdeveloped West,* p. 58.

⁵Goudzwaard, *Capitalism and Progress,* p. 193.

⁶*Technology: Abandon, Endure or Advance?* p. 12.

⁷*Pollution and the Death of Man: The Christian View of Ecology* (Wheaton, Ill.: Tyndale House, 1970), pp. 56-57.

⁸Compare Goudzwaard and Rifkin's discussion of Frederick Taylor's approach to scientific management in *Capitalism and Progress,* p. 92, and Rifkin, *Emerging Order,* pp. 186-89.

⁹Bell, *Cultural Contradictions of Capitalism,* p. 25.

¹⁰John Francis Kavanaugh describes ethical relativism as the "ethical embodiment of laissez faire economics" because it is noncommunitarian, isolationist, individualist, and because it espouses noninterference. *Following Christ in a Consumer Society* (Maryknoll, N.Y.: Orbis Books, 1981), p. 4.

¹Commenting on Daniel Bell's social analysis, Bernard Zylstra says, "Normative questions may indeed be raised but normative answers cannot be given" ("A Neoconservative Critique of Modernity," p. 354).

¹²Heilbroner, *An Inquiry into the Human Prospect,* pp. 131-32.

¹³Compare Goudzwaard, *Capitalism and Progress,* pp. 210-11.

¹⁴Ibid., pp. 65, 205. Goudzwaard attributes this insight to T. P. van der Kooy (footnote on p. 65).

¹⁵Ibid., p. 212.

¹⁶Ibid., p. 211.

¹⁷For a further discussion of the biblical model for economic life see Sider, *Rich Christians in an Age of Hunger,* part 2. More theoretical analysis can be found in Anthony Cramp, *Notes towards a Christian Critique of Secular Economic Theory* (Toronto: Institute for Christian Studies, 1975) and Alan Storkey, *A Christian Social Perspective* (Leicester, England:

Inter-Varsity Press, 1979), chaps. 13 and 14.

[18]Rifkin, *Emerging Order,* p. 269.

[19]Kavanaugh, *Following Christ in a Consumer Society,* p. 117.

Chapter 11: World View and Scholarship

[1]Hendrik Hart, "The Idea of an Inner Reformation of the Sciences" (Toronto: Institute for Christian Studies, 1980), p. 16.

[2]Of course, most governments that are influenced by this neoclassical approach are in fact inconsistent. Although they are noninterventionist in terms of regulating industry, they are interventionist when it comes to giving industry incentives and tax breaks. And in extreme cases they will even "bail out" floundering giants such as Chrysler Corporation.

[3]For helpful books dealing with behaviorism from a Christian perspective, see C. Stephen Evans, *Preserving the Person: A Look at the Human Sciences* (Downers Grove, Ill.: InterVarsity Press, 1977), chap. 4; Mary Stewart Van Leeuwen, *The Behaviourist Bandwagon and the Body of Christ* (Toronto: Institute for Christian Studies); and James W. Sire, "From the Bottom Up: World View Analysis as a Basis for Integration," in *Faith and Discipline* (Sterling, Kans.: Sterling College, 1980), esp. pp. 21-23.

[4]B. F. Skinner, *Beyond Freedom and Dignity* (New York: Vintage/Bantam, 1972), p. 193.

[5]Brian Walsh addressed this issue in his article "How to Think Your Way through College," *HIS* (November 1983).

[6]Evans, *Preserving the Person,* p. 18. See also David Lyon, *Christians and Sociology* (Downers Grove, Ill.: InterVarsity Press, 1975), p. 23; and Nancy Barcus, *Developing a Christian Mind* (Downers Grove, Ill.: InterVarsity Press, 1977), p. 23.

[7]Ian G. Barbour, *Issues in Science and Religion* (New York: Harper & Row, 1971), p. 151.

[8]Hendrik Hart, "Critical Reflections on Wolterstorff's *Reason within the Bounds of Religion*" (Toronto: Institute for Christian Studies, 1980), pp. 3-4.

[9]For a good introduction to Dooyeweerd's thought see his *In the Twilight of Western Thought* (Philadelphia: Presbyterian and Reformed, 1960), or *Roots of Western Culture.* His most extensive work can be found in his four-volume *A New Critique of Theoretical Thought,* trans. D. H. Freeman and W. S. Young (Philadephia: Presbyterian and Reformed, 1953-58). Much of our chapters 11 and 12 is dependent on material in an article written by Brian Walsh and Jon Chaplin, "Dooyeweerd's Contribution to a Christian Philosophical Paradigm," *Crux* 19, no. 1 (March 1983).

[10]See Sire, *Universe Next Door,* and his articles in *Faith and Discipline;* N. Wolterstorff, *Reason within the Bounds of Religion* (Grand Rapids, Mich.: Eerdmans, 1976); and Arthur Holmes, *All Truth Is God's Truth* (1977; reprint ed., Downers Grove, Ill.: InterVarsity Press, 1983).

[11]Thomas Kuhn, *The Structure of Scientific Revolutions,* rev. ed. (Chicago: Univ. of Chicago Press, 1962); N. R. Hanson, *Patterns of Discovery* (Cambridge: At the University Press, 1965); M. Polanyi, *Personal Knowledge* (Chicago: Univ. of Chicago Press, 1958); Gerard Radnitzky, *Contemporary Schools of Metascience* (Chicago: Henry Regnery Press, 1973).

[12]Barbour, *Issues in Science and Religion,* p. 139; Hanson, *Patterns of Discovery,* chap. 1.

[13]Dooyeweerd, *A New Critique,* 1:37.

[14]Sire, "From the Bottom Up," p. 27.

15Wolterstorff, *Reason within the Bounds of Religion,* pp. 62-63.

16Kuhn, *Structure of Scientific Revolutions,* pp. 147, 149-50, 157. Kuhn also compares a paradigm shift to a "gestalt" shift and argues that even perception is dependent on a preperceptual paradigm (pp. 112, 121). On perception see also Wolterstorff, *Reason within the Bounds of Religion,* p. 49; and Michael Polanyi, "The Scientific Revolution," in *Christians in a Technological Age,* ed. H. White (New York: Seabury Press, 1967), pp. 34-36. Concerning the relation between a paradigm and one's choice of scientific method, consider Paul Feyerabend's insightful comment: "Every methodological rule is associated with cosmological assumptions, so that using the rule we take it for granted that the assumptions are correct." Quoted by Alan Storkey in *A Christian Social Perspective* (Leicester, England: Inter-Varsity Press, 1979), p. 100.

17Holmes, *All Truth Is God's Truth,* p. 131.

18Evans, *Preserving the Person,* p. 66. For further discussion of functionalism see also Storkey, *A Christian Social Perspective,* pp. 52-56, 58-59, 64-66.

19Herman Dooyeweerd, *The Secularization of Science,* trans. R. Knudsen (Memphis: Christian Studies Center, 1979), p. 16.

20This is especially evident in Proverbs, Hosea and John. We are indebted to our colleague Hendrik Hart for much of the thought of this paragraph.

21This point has been made especially well in the writings of Michael Polanyi.

22Holmes, *All Truth Is God's Truth,* p. 125.

23Wolterstorff, *Reason within the Bounds of Religion,* p. 77.

24Ibid., p. 58.

Chapter 12: Toward a Christian Philosophical Framework

1This is what Herman Dooyeweerd calls the "cosmonomic idea." His philosophy is cosmonomic (in contrast with autonomous) because it deals with a cosmos which is subject to the law *(nomos)* of God, the Creator. Compare his *A New Critique of Theoretical Thought,* 1:93-113.

2Dooyeweerd, *Roots of Western Culture,* p. 153; Dooyeweerd's emphasis.

3For helpful discussions of the natural sciences/humanities distinction, compare Barbour, *Issues in Science and Religion,* chap. 7, and Wolfhart Pannenberg, *Theology and the Philosophy of Science,* trans. F. McDonagh (Philadelphia: Westminster Press, 1976), chap. 2.

4Donald MacKay, *The Clockwork Image* (Downers Grove, Ill.: InterVarsity Press, 1974), pp. 40-47. On p. 42, MacKay says, "Nothing-buttery is characterized by the notion that by reducing any phenomenon to its components you not only explain it, but *explain it away*"; MacKay's emphasis.

5For a helpful discussion of reductionistic understandings of the human person in the social sciences, see C. Stephen Evans, *Preserving the Person,* chaps. 1-5.

6See Dooyeweerd, *A New Critique of Theoretical Thought,* vol. 2.

7Alan Storkey, *A Christian Social Perspective,* pp. 132-33.

8The suggestions that follow are directed more to university or college students than to faculty members. Sire offers helpful suggestions in his article "How to Think Your Way through College," *HIS* (October 1981), p. 5.

9Unfortunately, many Christian professors live a dualistic life, leaving their Christian presuppositions at home before going to the laboratory or office.

A Bibliography We Can't Live Without

In this bibliography we have made a deliberate attempt not to be comprehensive. In most of the fields listed, there are many more books than the ones we have included. Rather than writing a comprehensive bibliography, we have attempted to compile the "bibliography we can't live without." These books are the essentials. Although we do not necessarily endorse everything that all of these books say, we nevertheless believe them to be foundational to developing a Christian perspective in each discipline.

The bibliography has three sections: (1) World Views and Cultural Analysis; (2) Natural and Applied Sciences and (3) The Humanities and Social Sciences. Section 1 is a list of resources with which everyone should be familiar. Sections 2 and 3 have subheadings for assorted disciplines offered at the university. Obviously, each of us needs to be reading the books in our own particular discipline.

We have also included a list of general books on "Christianity and science" and "Christianity and the humanities and social sciences" at the beginning of Sections 2 and 3 respectively. These books are helpful in getting a broader Christian perspective in our studies, which then must be worked out more specifically in each student's discipline.

All of the books in this bibliography are important. But to help students choose the *most* important books, we have placed an asterisk beside two or three entries under each subheading. If students cannot find time to read at least the asterisked books which are relevant to their studies, then they are probably not attempting to submit to the lordship of Christ in their studies. The books in this bibliography are foundational. Once the foundation has been set, we must build on it. We will need to search out other resources to help us be Christian students, integrated and whole.

1. World Views and Cultural Analysis
Distinctives of the Christian World View

Brown, Colin, ed. *New International Dictionary of New Testament Theology.* Grand Rapids, Mich.: Zondervan, 1978.

DeGraaff, Arnold, and Olthuis, James, eds. *Toward a Biblical View of Man: Some Readings.* Toronto, Institute for Christian Studies, 1978.

Fernhout, Harry. *Of Kings and Prophets: A Study of the Book of Kings.* Toronto, Curriculum Development Centre, 1979.

*Holmes, Arthur. *Contours of a Worldview.* Grand Rapids, Mich.: Eerdmans, 1983.

Kuyper, Abraham. *Lectures on Calvinism.* Grand Rapids, Mich.: Eerdmans, 1970.

*Ladd, George Eldon. *The Pattern of New Testament Truth.* Grand Rapids, Mich.: Eerdmans, 1968.

———. *A Theology of the New Testament.* Grand Rapids, Mich.: Eerdmans, 1974.

Macaulay, Ranald, and Barrs, Jerram. *Being Human: The Nature of Spiritual Experience.* Downers Grove, Ill.: InterVarsity Press, 1978.

Mouw, Richard J. *When the Kings Come Marching In.* Grand Rapids, Mich.: Eerdmans, 1984.

Seerveld, Calvin G. *Balaam's Apocalyptic Prophecies: A Study in Reading Scripture*. Toronto: Wedge, 1980.

Sinnema, Don. *Reclaiming the Land: A Study of the Book of Joshua*. Toronto: Curriculum Development Centre, 1977. (Teacher and Study Group edition)

Analysis of Western Culture

Dooyeweerd, Herman. *Roots of Western Culture: Pagan, Secular, and Christian Options*. Translated by J. Kraay. Toronto: Wedge, 1979.

Ellul, Jacques. *The Betrayal of the West*. New York: Seabury, 1978.

*Goudzwaard, Bob. *Capitalism and Progress: A Diagnosis of Western Society*. Translated by J. Van Nuis Zylstra. Grand Rapids, Mich.: Eerdmans, 1979.

*————. *Idols of Our Time*. Translated by M. VanderVennen. Downers Grove, Ill.: InterVarsity Press, 1984.

Guinness, Os. *The Dust of Death*. Downers Grove, Ill.: InterVarsity Press, 1973.

————. *The Gravedigger File: Papers on the Subversion of the Modern Church*. Downers Grove, Ill.: InterVarsity Press, 1983.

Hart, Hendrik. *The Challenge of Our Age*. Toronto: Wedge, 1974.

Rifkin, Jeremy (with Ted Howard). *The Emerging Order: God in the Age of Scarcity*. New York: Ballantine, 1979.

Comparison of World Views and Their Significance in University Studies

*Barcus, Nancy. *Developing a Christian Mind*. Downers Grove, Ill.: InterVarsity Press, 1977.

Blamires, Harry. *The Christian Mind*. Ann Arbor, Mich.: Servant, 1978.

Dickey, Douglas A. *What Else? Are There Really Any Acceptable Alternatives to Christianity?* Cincinnati: Standard Publishing Co., 1978.

Hermann, Ken. *University Study in Christian Perspective*. Toronto: Institute for Christian Studies, n.d.

*Niebuhr, H. Richard. *Christ and Culture*. New York: Harper & Row, 1983.

Sire, James W. *How to Read Slowly: A Guide to Reading with the Mind*. Downers Grove, Ill.: InterVarsity Press, 1978.

*————. *The Universe Next Door: A Basic World View Catalog*. Downers Grove, Ill.: InterVarsity Press, 1976.

Stevenson, Leslie. *Seven Theories of Human Nature*. New York: Oxford, 1974.

Stott, John R. W. *Your Mind Matters*. Downers Grove, Ill.: InterVarsity Press, 1973.

Wilkes, Peter, ed. *Christianity Challenges the University*. Downers Grove, Ill.: InterVarsity Press, 1981.

2. Natural and Applied Sciences

General Books on Understanding Science

*Barbour, Ian. *Issues in Science and Religion*. New York: Harper & Row, 1971.

Diemer, Johann H. *Nature and Miracle*. Toronto: Wedge, 1977.

Dooyeweerd, Herman. *The Secularization of Science*. Memphis, Tenn.: Christian Studies Center, 1954.

Gutting, Gary, ed. *Paradigms and Revolutions: Applications and Appraisals of Thomas Kuhn's Philosophy of Science*. Notre Dame, Ind.: Univ. of Notre Dame Press, 1980.

Hatfield, C., ed. *The Scientist and Ethical Decisions*. Downers Grove, Ill.: InterVarsity

Press, 1973.

Henry, Carl F., ed. *Horizons of Science: Christian Scholars Speak Out.* New York: Harper & Row, 1978.

*Hooykaas, R. *Religion and the Rise of Modern Science.* Grand Rapids, Mich.: Eerdmans, 1972.

Jaki, Stanley. *Cosmos and Creator.* Chicago: Regnery Gateway, 1982.

Jeeves, Malcolm. *The Scientific Enterprise and Christian Faith.* Downers Grove, Ill.: Inter-Varsity Press, 1969.

Kuhn, Thomas S. *The Structure of Scientific Revolutions.* 2d ed. Chicago: Univ. of Chicago Press, 1970.

*MacKay, Donald. *The Clockwork Image.* Downers Grove, Ill.: InterVarsity Press, 1974.

——— . *Human Science and Human Dignity.* Downers Grove, Ill.: InterVarsity Press, 1974.

Ramm, Bernard. *The Christian View of Science and Scripture.* Grand Rapids, Mich.: Eerdmans, 1954.

Biology (and the Evolution Debate)

Gillespie, Neal C. *Charles Darwin and the Problem of Creation.* Chicago: Univ. of Chicago Press, 1979.

*Greene, John C. *Science, Ideology and World View: Essays in the History of Evolutionary Ideas.* Berkeley: Univ. of Calif. Press, 1981.

Mixter, R. L. *Evolution and Christian Thought Today.* Grand Rapids, Mich.: Eerdmans.

Morris, H. *The Scientific Case for Creation.* San Diego: CLP Publications, 1977.

*Thurman, D. L. *How to Think about Evolution (and Other Bible-Science Controversies).* Downers Grove, Ill.: InterVarsity Press, 1978.

Wilder-Smith, A. E. *The Creation of Life.* Wheaton, Ill.: Harold Shaw, 1981.

——— . *Man's Origin, Man's Destiny.* Minneapolis: Bethany Fellowship, 1975.

Further material and resources:
Canadian Scientific and Christian Affiliation
P.O. Box 386
Fergus, Ontario, Canada N1M 3E2

Creation Research Society Quarterly
2717 Cranbrook Rd.
Ann Arbor, MI 48104

Creation, Social Science and Humanities Quarterly
1429 N. Holyoke
Wichita, KS 67208

The Journal of the American Scientific Affiliation
P.O. Box J
Ipswich, MA 01938
(Note: This journal deals with broader issues than just creation and evolution. It is a valuable resource for all of the disciplines.)

Geography and Environmental Studies

Elsdon, R. *Bent World*. Downers Grove, Ill.: InterVarsity Press, 1981.

Glacken, Clarence J. *Traces on the Rhodian Shore: Nature and Culture in Western Thought from Ancient Times to the End of the Eighteenth Century*. Berkeley: Univ. of Calif. Press, 1976.

Houston, James. *I Believe in the Creator*. Grand Rapids, Mich.: Eerdmans, 1979.

Schaeffer, Francis. *Pollution and the Death of Man*. Wheaton, Ill.: Tyndale House, 1969.

*Wilkinson, Loren, ed. *Earthkeeping: Christian Stewardship of Natural Resources*. Grand Rapids, Mich.: Eerdmans, 1980.

Physics

Dye, D. L. *Faith and the Physical World*. Grand Rapids, Mich.: Eerdmans.

Jaki, Stanley. *The Road of Science and the Ways of God*. Chicago: Univ. of Chicago Press, 1980.

MacKay, Donald, ed. *Christianity in a Mechanistic Universe*. Downers Grove, Ill.: Inter-Varsity Press, 1965.

*Owens, Virginia S. *And the Trees Clap Their Hands: Faith, Perception and the New Physics*. Grand Rapids, Mich.: Eerdmans, 1983.

Pollard, W. *Physicist and Christian*. Greenwich, Conn.: Seabury, 1961.

Stafleu, M. D. *Time and Again*. Toronto: Wedge, 1980.

Mathematics

Brabenec, R. L., et al. *A Christian Perspective on the Foundations of Mathematics*. Wheaton, Ill.: Wheaton College, 1977.

Granville, H., Jr. *Logos: Mathematics and Christian Theology*. E. Brunswick, N.J.: Bucknell Univ. Press, 1976.

Jongsma, Calvin. *The Shape and Number of Things*. Toronto: Curriculum Development Centre, 1981. (This is an exciting elementary school curriculum.)

Van Brummelen, Harro W. "The Place of Mathematics in the Curriculum," in *Shaping School Curriculum: A Biblical View*. Edited by G. Steensma. Terre Haute, Ind.: Signal Press, 1977.

Engineering

Ellul, Jacques. *The Technological Society*. New York: Random House, 1967.

Grant, George. *Technology and Empire*. Toronto: Anansi, 1969.

*Schumacher, E. F. *Small Is Beautiful*. New York: Harper & Row, 1976.

Schuurman, Egbert. *Technology and the Future*. Toronto: Wedge, 1980.

*————. *Reflections on the Technological Society*. Toronto: Wedge, 1977.

Medicine and Health Care

*Allen, D., Bird, C., and Hernmann, R., eds. *Whole-Person Medicine: An International Symposium*. Downers Grove, Ill.: InterVarsity Press, 1980.

Anderson, N. *Issues of Life and Death*. Kent, England: Hodder & Stoughton, 1978.

Fish, S., and Shelly, J. A. *Spiritual Care: The Nurse's Role*. Downers Grove, Ill.: InterVarsity Press, 1978.

*Jones, D. Gareth. *Our Fragile Brains*. Downers Grove, Ill.: InterVarsity Press, 1980.

Koop, C. Everett. *Right to Live, Right to Die*. Wheaton, Ill.: Tyndale House, 1976.

Nelson, J. B. *Human Medicine*. Minneapolis: Augsburg, 1973.

Ramsey, Paul. *Fabricated Man*. New Haven, Conn.: Yale Univ. Press, 1970.

Shelly, Judith A. *Dilemma: A Nurse's Guide for Making Ethical Decisions.* Downers Grove,
   Ill.: InterVarsity Press, 1980.
Thomas, J. E. *Matters of Life and Death: Crises in Bio-Medical Ethics.* Sarasota, Fla.: Samuel
   Stevens Press, 1978.
Food, Nutrition and Agriculture
Lappé, Frances M., and Collins, Joseph. *Food First.* New York: Ballantine, 1977.
*Longacre, D. Janzen. *Living More with Less.* Scottdale, Penn.: Herald Press, 1980.
——— . "Introduction," in *More-with-Less Cookbook.* Scottdale, Penn.: Herald Press, 1976.
McGinnis, J. *Bread and Justice.* Ramsey, N.J.: Paulist Press, 1979.
Nelson, J. A. *Hunger for Justice.* Maryknoll, N.Y.: Orbis Books, 1980.
*Simon, Arthur. *Bread for the World.* Grand Rapids, Mich.: Eerdmans, 1975.

   Further material and resources:
   The Christian Farmer
   Christian Farmer's Federation
   Box 698
   Harriston, Ontario, Canada N0G 1Z0

   From Swords to Plowsnares
   Box 347
   Newton, KS 67114

   Plow-Share
   Christian Farmer's Federation of Western Canada
   10766 - 97 St.
   Edmonton, Alberta, Canada T5H 2M1

Note: Agriculture students should also pay attention to books listed under "Geography and Environmental Studies" above.

3. The Humanities and Social Sciences
**General Books Setting a Christian Foundation for Studies in the Humanities and
Social Sciences**
Berkouwer, G. C. *Man: The Image of God.* Studies in Dogmatics, vol. 8. Translated by
   D. Jellema. Grand Rapids, Mich.: Eerdmans, 1962.
DeGraff, Arnold, and Olthuis, James, eds. *Towards a Biblical View of Man: Some Read-
   ings.* Toronto: Institute for Christian Studies, 1978.
*Evans, C. Stephen. *Preserving the Person.* Downers Grove, Ill.: InterVarsity Press, 1977.
Guinness, Os. *The Dust of Death.* Downers Grove, Ill.: InterVarsity Press, 1973.
*Macaulay, Ranald, and Barrs, Jerram. *Being Human: The Nature of Spiritual Experience.*
   Downers Grove, Ill.: InterVarsity Press, 1978.
Schrotenboer, Paul. *Man in God's World.* Toronto: Wedge, 1977.
Philosophy
Brown, Colin. *Philosophy and the Christian Faith.* Downers Grove, Ill.: InterVarsity Press,
   1969.

Dooyeweerd, Herman. *In the Twilight of Western Thought.* Nutley, N.J.: Craig Press, 1968.
*Hart, Hendrik. *Understanding Our World.* Washington, D.C.: University Press of America, 1984.
Holmes, Arthur, *All Truth Is God's Truth.* Downers Grove, Ill.: InterVarsity Press, 1983.
————. *Philosophy: A Christian Perspective.* Downers Grove, Ill.: InterVarsity Press, 1975.
Kalsbeek, L. *Contours of a Christian Philosophy.* Toronto: Wedge, 1975.
Wolfe, David L. *Epistemology: The Justification of Belief.* Downers Grove, Ill.: InterVarsity Press, 1982.
*Wolters, Albert. *Our Place in the Philosophical Tradition.* Toronto: Institute for Christian Studies, 1975.
*Wolterstorff, Nicholas. *Reason within the Bounds of Religion.* Grand Rapids, Mich.: Eerdmans, 1976.

Further resources:
Faith and Philosophy
Journal of the Society of Christian Philosophers
Dept. of Philosophy
Asbury College
Wilmore, KY 40390

Religious Studies

Anderson, J. N. D., ed. *The World's Religions.* Grand Rapids, Mich.: Eerdmans, 1976.
Childs, Brevard. *Introduction to the Old Testament as Scripture.* Philadelphia: Fortress, 1979.
Gabelein, F., ed. *Expositor's Bible Commentary,* vol. 1. Grand Rapids, Mich.: Zondervan, 1979.
Kitchen, K. A. *Ancient Orient and Old Testament.* Downers Grove, Ill.: InterVarsity Press, 1966.
*Kline, Meredith. *The Structure of Biblical Authority.* Grand Rapids, Mich.: Eerdmans, 1972.
Ladd, George Eldon. *The New Testament and Criticism.* Grand Rapids, Mich.: Eerdmans, 1967.
Malony, H. Newton. *Current Perspectives in the Psychology of Religion.* Grand Rapids, Mich.: Eerdmans, 1977.
*Olthuis, James H. *Visions of Life and Ways of Life: The Nature of Religion.* Toronto: Institute for Christian Studies, n.d.
Ridderbos, Herman. *Paul: An Outline of His Theology.* Translated by J. R. deWitt. Grand Rapids, Mich.: Eerdmans, 1975.
*Thiselton, Anthony. *The Two Horizons: New Testament Hermeneutics and Philosophical Description with Special Reference to Heidegger, Bultmann, Gadamer, and Wittgenstein.* Grand Rapids, Mich.: Eerdmans, 1980.
Yoder, Perry. *From Word to Life: A Guide to the Art of Bible Study.* Scottdale, Penn.: Herald Press, 1982.

Further resources:
Themelios
Theological Students Fellowship
233 Langdon St.
Madison, WI 53703

Crux
2130 Wesbrook Mall
Vancouver, British Columbia, Canada V6T 1W6

Journal of the Evangelical Theological Society
c/o S. J. Kristemacher
Reformed Theological Seminary
5422 Clinton Blvd.
Jackson, MS 39209

Apologetics

Bruce, F. F. *The New Testament Documents: Are They Reliable?* 5th ed. Downers Grove, Ill.: InterVarsity Press, 1960.

Geehan, E. R., ed. *Jerusalem and Athens: Critical Discussions on the Philosophy and Apologetics of Cornelius Van Til.* Philadelphia: Presbyterian and Reformed, 1977.

Lewis, C. S. *Mere Christianity.* New York: Macmillan, 1981.

Lewis, Gordon. *Testing Christianity's Truth Claims: Approaches to Christian Apologetics.* Chicago: Moody Press, 1980.

Pinnock, Clark. *Reason Enough.* Downers Grove, Ill.: InterVarsity Press, 1980.

*Ramm, Bernard. *Varieties of Christian Apologetics.* Grand Rapids, Mich.: Baker Book House, 1974.

Reid, J. K. S. *Christian Apologetics.* Grand Rapids, Mich.: Eerdmans, 1969.

Schaeffer, Francis. *The God Who Is There.* Downers Grove, Ill.: InterVarsity Press, 1968.

History

*Bebbington, D. W. *Patterns in History.* Downers Grove, Ill.: InterVarsity Press, 1980.

Butterfield, Herbert. *Man on His Past: The Study of History of Historical Scholarship.* Cambridge: At the Univ. Press, 1969.

*————. *Writings on Christianity and History.* Edited by C. T. McIntire. New York: Oxford, 1979.

Gilkey, Langdon. *Reaping the Whirlwind: A Christian Interpretation of History.* New York: Seabury, 1977.

Marsden, George, and Roberts, Frank, eds. *A Christian View of History?* Grand Rapids, Mich.: Eerdmans, 1975.

McIntire, C. Thomas. *The Focus of Historical Study: A Christian View.* Toronto: Institute for Christian Studies, n.d.

*————, ed. *God, History and Historians.* New York: Oxford, 1977.

Niebuhr, Reinhold. *Faith and History: A Comparison of Christian and Modern Views of History.* New York: Scribner's, 1949.

Further resources:
Fides et Historia
c/o Secretary, Conference on Faith and History
Dept. of History, Indiana State University
Terre Haute, IN 47809

Psychology

Collins, Gary. *The Rebuilding of Psychology*. Wheaton, Ill.: Tyndale House, 1977.
DeGraaff, Arnold. *Psychology: Sensitive Openness and Appropriate Reactions*. Toronto: Institute for Christian Studies, n.d.
————, ed. *Views of Man and Psychology: Readings in Psychology and Christianity*. Toronto: Institute for Christian Studies, n.d.
Evans, C. Stephen. *Preserving the Person*. Downers Grove, Ill.: InterVarsity Press, 1977.
Jeeves, Malcolm. *Psychology and Christianity: The View Both Ways*. Downers Grove, Ill.: InterVarsity Press, 1976.
Knudsen, R. D. *Psychology: The Encounter of Christianity with Secular Science*. Memphis, Tenn.: Christian Studies Center, n.d.
*Myers, David. *The Human Puzzle: Psychological Research and Christian Belief*. New York: Harper & Row, 1978.
Tournier, Paul. *The Meaning of Persons*. New York: Harper & Row, 1982.
Van Leeuwen, Mary Stewart. *Christianity and Psychology*. Grand Rapids, Mich.: Eerdmans, 1984.
*————. *The Sorcerer's Apprentice*. Downers Grove, Ill.: InterVarsity Press, 1983.

Further resources:
The Bulletin of the Christian Association for Psychological Studies
c/o 2675 Farmington Rd.
Farmington Hill, MI 48018

Sociology

Catherwood, H. F. R. *The Christian in Industrial Society*. London: Tyndale Press, 1966.
De Santo, C. *Christian Perspectives on Social Problems*. Scottdale, Penn.: Herald Press, 1983.
De Santo, C.; Smith-Hinds, W.; and Redekop, C. *A Reader in Sociology: Christian Perspectives*. Scottdale, Penn.: Herald Press, 1980.
Gladwin, John. *God's People in God's World: Biblical Motives for Social Involvement*. Downers Grove, Ill.: InterVarsity Press, 1980.
Goudzwaard, Bob. *Aid for the Overdeveloped West*. Toronto: Wedge, 1975.
Grunlan, Stephen, and Reimer, M., eds. *Christian Perspective on Sociology*. Grand Rapids, Mich.: Zondervan, 1982.
Knudsen, Robert D. *Sociology: The Encounter of Christianity with Secular Science*. Memphis, Tenn.: Christian Study Center, 1981.
*Lyon, David. *Christians and Sociology*. Downers Grove, Ill.: InterVarsity Press, 1975.
*Storkey, Alan. *A Christian Social Perspective*. Leicester, England: Inter-Varsity Press, 1979.

Further resources:
Christian Sociologist
c/o George Hillary
Virginia Polytechnical Institute
Blackburg, VA 24061

National Association for Christians in Social Work
P.O. Box 84
Wheaton, IL 60187

Note: People in sociology and social work should also pay attention to the resoι rces listed under "Psychology," "Political Studies" and "Economics."

Economics and Commerce

Antonides, Harry. *Multinationals and the Peaceable Kingdom*. Toronto: Clark Irwin, 1978.

Cramp, A. B. *Notes toward a Christian Critique of Secular Economic Theory*. Toronto: Institute for Christian Studies, n.d.

Ellul, Jacques. *Money and Power*. Translated by LaVonne Neff. Downers Grove, Ill.: Inter-Varsity Press, 1984.

*Goudzwaard, Bob. *Capitalism and Progress: A Diagnosis of Western Society*. Grand Rapids, Mich.: Eerdmans, 1979.

Griffiths, Brian. *Christianity and Economics*. Grand Rapids, Mich.: Eerdmans, forthcoming.

Justice in the International Economic Order. Proceedings of the 2nd Conference for Christian Higher Education. Grand Rapids, Mich.: Calvin College, 1980.

Schumacher, E. F. *Small Is Beautiful: Economics As If People Mattered*. New York: Harper & Row, 1976.

*Sider, Ronald J. *Rich Christians in an Age of Hunger*. 2d ed., rev. Downers Grove, Ill.: InterVarsity Press, 1977.

Wogaman, John Philip. *The Great Economic Debate: An Ethical Analysis*. Philadelphia: Westminster, 1977.

Note: People in economics and commerce should also pay attention to the resources listed under "Sociology" and "Political Studies."

Political Studies

Dooyeweerd, Herman. *The Christian Idea of the State*. Philadelphia: Presbyterian and Reformed, 1967.

Ellul, Jacques. *The Politics of God and the Politics of Man*. Grand Rapids, Mich.: Eerdmans, 1972.

Goudzwaard, Bob. *A Christian Political Option*. Toronto: Wedge, 1972.

Lyon, David. *Karl Marx: A Christian Assessment of His Life and Thought*. Downers Grove, Ill.: InterVarsity Press, 1979.

*Malloch, Ted, and Harper, William A., eds. *Where Are We Now? The State of Christian

Political Reflection. Washington, D.C.: University Press of America, 1981.

Marshall, Paul. *Thine Is the Kingdom: A Biblical Perspective on Government and Politics Today*. London: Marshall, Morgan and Scott, 1984.

Mott, Stephen C. *Biblical Ethics and Social Change*. New York: Oxford, 1982.

*Mouw, R. J. *Politics and the Biblical Drama*. Grand Rapids, Mich.: Baker Book House, 1983.

Nash, Ronald H. *Social Justice and the Christian Church*. Milford, Mich.: Mott Media, 1983.

*Wolterstorff, Nicholas. *Until Justice and Peace Embrace*. Grand Rapids, Mich.: Eerdmans, 1984.

Yoder, John Howard. *The Politics of Jesus*. Grand Rapids, Mich.: Eerdmans, 1972.

Further resources:
Christian Labour Association of Canada
(publishes *The Guide*)
821 Albion Rd.
Toronto, Ontario, Canada M9V 1A1

Citizens for Public Justice
(publishes *Catalyst*)
229 College St.
Toronto, Ontario, Canada M5T 1R4

Note: Students in political studies should also pay attention to resources listed under "Sociology" and "Economics."

The following journals are helpful for people in sociology, political studies and economics:
Sojourners
1398 L St. NW
Washington, D.C. 20005

The Other Side
300 Apsley St.
Philadelphia, PA 19144

Reformed Journal
255 Jefferson SE
Grand Rapids, MI 49503

Christian Scholar's Review
RD 2
Union, ME 04862

Radix
P.O. Box 2116
Berkeley, CA 94702

(Note that these journals are broadly interdisciplinary and therefore contain articles which are of relevance to many other disciplines and interests.)

Art and Aesthetics

DeVries, Daniel. *The Films of Stanley Kubrick*. Grand Rapids, Mich.: Eerdmans, 1973.

Drew, Donald J. *Images of Man: A Critique of Contemporary Cinema*. Downers Grove, Ill.: InterVarsity Press, 1974.

Rookmaaker, Hans. *The Creative Gift: Essays on Art and Christian Life*. Westchester, Ill.: Good News, 1981.

———. *Modern Art and the Death of a Culture*. Downers Grove, Ill.: InterVarsity Press, 1970.

*Ryken, Leland, ed. *The Christian Imagination*. Grand Rapids, Mich.: Baker Book House, 1981.

Schaeffer, Francis. *Art and the Bible*. Downers Grove, Ill.: InterVarsity Press, 1973.

Seerveld, Calvin G. *A Christian Critique of Art and Literature*. Toronto: Wedge, 1976.

*———. *Rainbows for the Fallen World*. Beaver Falls, Penn.: Radix Books, 1980.

*Wolterstorff, Nicholas. *Art in Action*. Grand Rapids, Mich.: Eerdmans, 1980.

———. *Christianity and Art*. Grand Rapids, Mich.: Eerdmans, forthcoming.

Literature

Ericson, E. E., and Tennyson, G. B., eds. *Religion and Modern Literature: Essays in Theory and Criticism*. Grand Rapids, Mich.: Eerdmans.

*Jeffries, David. *Christianity and Literature*. Grand Rapids, Mich.: Eerdmans, forthcoming.

Lewis, C. S. *Studies in Words*. Cambridge: At the Univ. Press, 1974.

O'Connor, Flannery. *Mystery and Manners*. New York: Farrar, Straus & Giroux, 1969.

*Ryken, Leland. *Triumphs of the Imagination*. Downers Grove, Ill.: InterVarsity Press, 1979.

Sayers, Dorothy. *The Mind of the Maker*. New York: Harper & Row, 1979.

TeSelle, S. F. *Literature and the Christian Life*. New Haven: Yale, 1966.

Zylstra, Henry. *Testament of Vision*. Grand Rapids, Mich.: Eerdmans, 1961.

Further resources:
Christianity and Literature
c/o English Dept., Calvin College
Grand Rapids, MI 49506

Note: People in music would find assistance in some of the books listed under "Art and Aesthetics" and "Literature."

Education

Freire, P. *Pedagogy of the Oppressed*. New York: Continuum, 1970.

Holmes, Arthur. *The Idea of a Christian College*. Grand Rapids, Mich.: Eerdmans, 1975.

*Malcolm, Tom, and Fernhout, Harry. *Education and the Public Purpose*. Toronto: Curriculum Development Centre, n.d.

Martin, Charles. *You've Got to Start Somewhere . . . When You Think about Education*.

Leicester, England: Inter-Varsity Press, 1979.

*Steensma, Geraldine, and Van Brummelen, Harro, eds. *Shaping School Curriculum: A Biblical View*. Terre Haute, Ind.: Signal Press, 1977.

Wolterstorff, Nicholas. *Educating for Responsible Action*. Grand Rapids, Mich.: Eerdmans, 1982.

Further resources:
Curriculum Development Centre
229 College St.
Toronto, Ontario, Canada M5T 1R4
(This organization has written curriculum materials for elementary, junior high and high school from a Christian perspective. It also publishes a newsletter.)